AF572316

The French Literary Filmmakers

Other Books by John J. Michalczyk

André Malraux's Film Espoir*: The Propaganda/Art Film and the Spanish Civil War*

Ingmar Bergman: La Passion d'être homme aujourd'hui (in French)

The French Literary Filmmakers

John J. Michalczyk

Philadelphia: The Art Alliance Press
London and Toronto: Associated University Presses

Associated University Presses, Inc.
Cranbury, New Jersey 08512

Associated University Presses
Magdalen House
136-148 Tooley Street
London SE1 2TT, England

Associated University Presses
Toronto M5E 1A7, Canada

Library of Congress Cataloging in Publication Data

Michalczyk, John J 1941-
The French literary filmmakers.

Filmography: p.
Bibliography: p.
Includes index.
1. Moving-picture producers and directors—France. 2. Film adaptations. 3. Moving-pictures—France. 4. French literature—Film adaptations.
I Title.
PN1993.5.F7M48 791.43'023'0922 78-75171
ISBN 0-87982-027-6

Printed in the United States of America

To my mother Sophie,
who lovingly embodies the "wisdom"
of the old and the new worlds.

CONTENTS

ACKNOWLEDGMENTS

A very tangible, physical object such as this literary work is the end product of a long, complex, but interrelated series of encounters over the space of three years. I reflect my indebtedness here for the very intangible but memorable encounters with the following individuals or groups:

Académie française (Archives)
American Society Legion of Honor Magazine
Patrick Baliani (Boston College)
Ciné Minotaure (Photo Library)
Cinémathèque française (Photos)
Community of La Baume Sainte-Marie
Henri Fleuchère (*Bulletin des Amis de Jean Giono*)
Emmanuel Flipo (International Film and Television Council)
Joseph Gauthier, S.J. (Boston College)
Aline Giono (Daughter of the Novelist)
I.D.H.E.C. (Cinema Institute Library, Paris)
Jesuit Community of Boston College
Jesuit Community of Centre Sèvres, Paris
Henri Langlois †
Walter Langlois (University of Wyoming, Editor of *Mélanges Malraux Miscellany*)
André Malraux †
Denis Marion (assistant to Malraux for *Espoir*)
James McCann (Centre Sèvres, Paris)
Claire Murray (Arthur D. Little, Inc.)
René Pagnol (Brother of the Filmmaker)
Susan Ross (Boston College)
Russell Young and the Fondation Camargo (Cassis, France)
François Villiers (Director of *L'Eau vive*)
Christopher Willcock (Centre Sèvres)

The chapter on Robbe-Grillet has been published in part in *American Society Legion of Honor Magazine*, vol. 48, no. 1 (1977).

PREVIEWS

A pebble cast into the stagnant waters of the French film industry in the late 1950s created ripples of concentric circles that soon landed on international shores . . .the beginnings of the "Nouvelle Vague." The New Wave—a term coined by Françoise Giroud to describe the young generation of 1957-1958—was represented by the young rebel filmmakers Rohmer, Truffaut, Godard, Resnais, and Chabrol, and it would soon leave its indelible mark on the film world. A modest budget, a sense of spontaneity and experimentation, casts of little-known actors, and a portrayal of social realism that tended toward "cinéma vérité"—these are the characteristics of a budding movement that now serves as a landmark in the history of modern cinema.

The New Wave was not the only significant phenomenon in the film world of the late 1950s and early 1960s. During this short period the two spheres of literature and cinema were fruitfully interacting to create new dimensions in artistic expression. It was, first of all, from the realm of film criticism that this controversial movement was born. Truffaut, Rivette, Chabrol, Godard, and Doniol-Valcroze—all rising from the academic ranks of André Bazin at the budding popular journal *Cahiers du Cinéma*—wielded first the pen and then the camera. Later, on occasion, they would put aside the camera to return to film theory that they disseminated once again through the vehicle of cinema journals.

The well-established Cannes Film Festival even condescended to meet the littérateurs halfway. For three successive years a casual nod was made in their direction:

1959 *Hiroshima, mon amour*, from a script by Marguerite Duras, Resnais's first feature film and the beginning of a long line of collaborative ventures, shocked, bored, and intellectually stimulated the public and press, and was then rewarded with a prize. The same reaction would occur in Venice for *Marienbad* in 1961. The New Wave, recognized at both festivals, gathered momentum.

1960 The literary world was represented by André Malraux, Raymond Queneau, and Henry Miller. With the projection of *Le Testament d'Orphée* of Cocteau, homage was rendered the poet/cinéaste.

1961 An author—Jean Giono—was chosen president of the jury. Another script from Marguerite Duras brought the resulting film, Colpi's *Une aussi longue absence*, to the festival.

The "Immortals" of the Académie française, the celebrated institution of brilliant high priests, also recognized the importance of the new Muse "Cinéma." To their ranks they invited René Clair in 1960, the first time that a filmmaker without a professional literary background such as that of Marcel Pagnol and Jean Cocteau was elected to the prestigious world of the more than 300-year-old academy.

During this brief period of 1959-1961, the authors treated in this work—aside from the playwright/cinéaste Sacha Guitry (who died in (1957)—were still living and were in some way or other affiliated with the cinema. Malraux, the minister of culture, manifested his concern for the direction of the Cinémathèque, for film censorship, and for film education in 1959 and 1960. Robbe-Grillet had planned the film *L'Immortelle* before he undertook the script for the controversial *Marienbad* (1961). The literary works of the Academician Pagnol were being adapted for television, his films were shown in revivals and festivals, and his theater pieces were staged with a tinge of nostalgia. At the same time, Giono was collaborating with several directors in the adaptation of his novels and filmed *Crésus* in 1961. Marguerite Duras's original contacts with the world of literature were via the novel and theater; after furnishing a script for Resnais's *Hiroshima* (1959) and Colpi's *Une aussi longue absence* (1961), she began to film her own plays and novels. Cocteau in 1960 completed his *Testament d'Orphée* and contributed to the *Cahiers du Cinéma* in art and literature on occasion, especially for its one hundreth issue for which he designed a jubilant muse looking at a reel of celluloid.

Symbiotic in nature and fecund in results, this cinema/literature relationship of the late 1950s and early 1960s marked a new golden age in the history of the two media that had already witnessed an eleven-minute *Faust* of Méliès at the turn of the century, the fragile epoch of the *théâtre filmé* in the 1930s and Bresson's soul-searing rendition of Bernanos's novel *Journal d'un curé de campagne* in 1950, the epitome of adaptations.

In analyzing our pleiad of filmmakers, who have as their ancestors in number and intention the seven sixteenth-century poetic innovators Ronsard, Du Bellay, Dorat, Belleau, Jodelle, Baïf, and de Tyard, we will attempt to re-create their respective universe of film and see the correlation of these two means of aesthetic composition, which will be shown to dovetail. These contemporary artists, who primarily have created an international reputation first in literature and then in cinema, comprise neither a school nor a movement, but very significantly, they share in common an openness to a fresh vision as expressed in the medium of film.

Telescoped plots, the particular themes represented in each film, and a commentary on the individual work and the history of its origin will assist in the development of the very personal world of the novelist who allows himself or herself to be drawn further and further into the milieu of cinema. Cocteau's magical mystery tour through myth and legend, the boulevardier Guitry's "soap opera" on celluloid, Pagnol's colorful saga of the Mediterranean world, Giono's ecological return to nature, Malraux's *cinéma engagé*, Robbe-Grillet's esoteric eroticism, and Duras's lyrical and cerebral phantasms—the diversity of expression originating in these artists can hardly be matched. Neither black nor white, the gray segment of fertile collaboration in the French art world will further reveal a vast range of discernible nuances.

The French Literary Filmmakers

1

JEAN COCTEAU

Long live the young Muse "Cinéma," for she has access to the mysteries of the dream world and can make the unreal appear real.

(1959)

Once upon a time when Paris was still yesterday and the ox was on the roof with the *enfants terribles* lurking in the corridors of the Lycée Condorcet below,[1] there lived a poet, or at least he said he was a poet. (Quod scripsit, scripsit!) Not unlike the oracle of Delphi, he would utter arcane verses that enchanted his friends, infuriated the critics, and left the uninitiated public in the uncomfortable dark. When his divine musings became *à la mode*, and the Immortals were in need of a court jester, he was invited to play his *violon d'Ingres* for the savants in attendance. There along the murky river of Babylon he continued to perform in veiled language gifted by the company of his Muses. Enigmatically he would chant about the calling of a poet seduced by love and death until that fateful day when Death herself came to claim the poet and the poetess Edith, to make of them cultic objects of a poetic religion.[2]

And so would Jean Cocteau's tale be told from generation to generation with fiction and reality side by side like unsifted wheat and chaff. Some bearers of the legend would be jealous of his kaleidoscopic talents, frustrated in their inability to pigeonhole the creative genius of this "Fregoli," or repulsed by his eclecticism or his cavalier, demythologizing attitude about intellectual pursuits. For them he would be the "Jean-of-all-trades," but master of none. Others would be able to penetrate the mirror of appearances and see in Cocteau a fertile spirit that crossed many movements (cubism, modernism, fauvism, expressionism, Orphism, dadaism, surrealism, and futurism) but left each in the dust of his next creative undertaking.

When André Maurois formally welcomed Jean Cocteau into the bosom of the Académie française on 20 October 1955, he underscored the sacredness of the poet's vocation in these terms:

> Above all you are a "poet," and you rightly attach to this word a meaning infinitely more extensive than simply "an author of works in verse." You call your work: poetry of the novel, poetry of criticism, poetry of the theatre. For yourself, just as for Valéry, a poet is a mythmaker who, with his charms, clarifies beyond appearances the mystery and beauty of this world. By the rhythms, by the choice of words, by the clarification of details before him that are invisible, and by the intimate juxaposition of the most concrete reality with the "sur-real," the poet recreates the universe. When the poet does this, as you do with all of your very being, he also creates his own life.[3]

With these select words, Maurois, before summarizing the films and other aesthetic achievements of the artist, acknowledged Jean Cocteau as a veritable poet, a creator of myths who weaved his personal "sacred tale" in the blending of colorful, mysterious levels of existence and in doing so recreated his own poetic *élan vital.* Maurois clearly comprehends Cocteau's true vocation.

Cocteau's is a fragile, complex world enshrined under glass, on exhibit for all to view but not to touch. For a brief second we dare to lift the glass encasement to peer underneath, to feel, and to examine. His works that follow are easier to enumerate than to decipher, but let us accept the challenge of both tasks.

Jean Cocteau was but a six-year-old prodigy when Lumière brought the new art of cinema into the world, with his on-the-spot filming of the exit of the employees from the Lyons factory, the train arriving at La Ciotat, the sprinkling prank, and the young children playing at the seaside. The last mentioned would be one of the earliest films Cocteau would recall seeing, although he would eventually view the others. Growing up in the glitter of stage life and nourished by the exotic trends of the Belle Epoque, Cocteau would not have long to wait before he could indulge in the comic films of Chaplin, Keaton, and Langdon, when the childlike art of the film was still speechless. Little did the young Cocteau realize then that the great "Charlot" and he would eventually meet on board ship during Cocteau's trip around the world in 1936. Chaplin and Cocteau would become friends and later exchange letters in a lighthearted fashion. Cocteau's perspicacious comment about the American comic would certainly apply to himself: "He is a very engaging man, obsessed with his own personality."[4]

Cocteau took into his personal film world not the tone of the entertaining films of the tragicomic vagabond but the more serious works from the silent era, especially of the late 1920s and then the early 1930s. Despite Franco-Germanic hostilities, the German expressionist films were very popular with the French intellectuals, especially those who, like Malraux,-witnessed the "fantastic" films during their travels in Germany. In Cocteau's cinematic hall of fame the heroes Murnau, Wiene, Lang, and Lubitsch would take their honored places. He would be profoundly moved by Dreyer's *Passion de Jeanne d'Arc* and Eisenstein's *Potemkin.* A William S. Hart film and another called *Forfaiture* (1937) would, however, leave the greatest impression on the young Cocteau.

While breathing the revolutionary air of surrealism, the inventive cinéastes of the 1920s dabbled in experimentation that would pave the way for Cocteau. Germaine Dulac's *La Coquille et le clergyman*, from the scenario by the brilliant—and deranged—theoretician, poet, and stage director Antonin Artaud; René Clair's *Entr'acte;* Fernand Leger's futuristic *Ballet mécanique*; and Jean Vigo's *Zéro de conduite* (precursor of *400 Coups* and *If*) set the tone of the nonconformist cinema—already a quarter of a century old, but a toddler in respect to the history of the other arts. A flurry of imagination and eccentricity, antiestablishment innuendos, and bizarre juxtapositions with an exhilarating freedom of expression characterized these early films. Cocteau's initial ventures in cinema would be in much the same vein.

Controversy engenders controversy. Following the 1928 scandal of the Buñuel/Dali film *Un Chien andalou*, Buñuel's *L'Age d'or* and Cocteau's *Le Sang d'un poète* soon produced another polemic. In 1930, with the generosity of a Maecenas sponsoring a Vergil or a Horace, the vicomte Charles de Noailles offered Buñuel and Cocteau a million francs each and carte blanche to make two films. The Spanish cinéaste went about his task producing the anticlerical and antibourgeois *L'Age d'or*, which immediately brought down the wrath of the various representatives of society. The infamous reputation of this film, Cocteau mentioned on occasion, would be confused with his own less controversial and more lyrical *Le Sang d'un poète.*

De Noailles originally requested Cocteau—already established as the prince among the youth especially for his novel *Les Enfants terribles* (1929)—to make an animated film. Realizing that he would need a large crew of assistants, more technical know-how, and a factory to produce the work, Cocteau compromised and created *Le Sang d'un poète* that he would consider an animated film with live people, just like the *tableaux vivants* ("living paintings") at a fair. Michel Arnaud was by his side to provide the technical assistance, and Georges Auric, one of "les Six," furnished the musical composition for the film. Although not an animated film in the strict sense of the word, certain sequences, for instance that of the prostrate hermaphrodite with a swirling disk and labeled "Danger de Mort," could leap right out of an animated work. In his first venture, Cocteau—the freethinker and rule bender that he was—fabricated his own cinematic language as he went along, opposed to the academic principles of cinema.

With no film experience, save perhaps for the sixteen mm film venture in 1925, *Jean Cocteau fait un film*, Cocteau "invented" a voyage into the beyond under the influence of Chaplin—and not opium this time. When a filmmaker terminates a work of art both his soul and his aesthetic vision become engraved on celluloid. For Cocteau in *Le Sang d'un poète* this was certainly the case. This life and death of a poet surrounded like bookends by the collapse of a large chimney (described as phallic by some young girls in a mental hospital, observed the poet[5]), was introduced by the cinéaste's message: "Every poem is a coat of arms which must be deciphered."[6]

Four episodes in the film recount the poet's odyssey toward death:

1. "The wounded hand or the scars of the poet." (Shades of *Un Chien andalou!*)
2. "Do the walls have ears?" (A visit to the Hôtel des Folies)
3. "The snowball fight." (A scene from *Les Enfants terribles*)
4. "The stolen card: the profanation of the host." (A souvenir from an Uccello painting, also mentioned in Breton's *Nadja*)

In *Le Sang d'un poète* Cocteau would literally create from the dust of the studio floor, filming in the diaphanous light, fashioning a second horn for the asymmetrical ox, designing the quasi-surrealist sets, and narrating his commentary. The vicomte de Noailles and his wife would often pass by the studio to watch the progress of their "investment." Cocteau on one occasion asked if they would like to participate in the film. They agreed and were filmed chatting and applauding in the theater box. Cocteau's patrons were much dismayed when they found themselves after the final editing applauding a suicide. Cocteau remade the controversial scene with Barbette, the American circus transvestite, and extras in place of the de Noailles. The film, however, certainly did not advance the reputation of the nobles who suffered a lethal blow in the social realm for the sponsorship of the Buñuel and Cocteau enterprises.

Cocteau has always been considered in the history of French literature *en marge du Surréalisme*, and although at odds with the stalwart members of the movement he eventually became reconciled with them before his death, except in the case of Breton.[7] In filming *Le Sang d'un poète* Cocteau incorporated elements that were very precious to the surrealists with strange juxtapositions: a card game on the body of the young, wounded lad; a child chained next to a fireplace; statues coming alive; water boiling when the hand of the poet is inserted therein; and a voyage through the zone of the mirror, used again in *Orphée* and *Le Testament d'Orphée*. Though not as shocking as the slicing of a young lady's eyeball with a razor in the first sequence of Buñuel's *Un Chien andalou*, Cocteau's *Sang* still created controversies whenever it was presented in the 1930s. In discussing the film with André Fraigneau, Cocteau said that he was not influenced by Buñuel in any way since both *Le Sang* and *L'Age d'or* were filmed simultaneously at a great distance from each other, and only later did Buñuel screen *Un Chien andalou* for Cocteau.[8]

Fraigneau was accurate when he called the Cocteau film "archetypal," and the filmmaker himself felt that Freud's interpretation of the film was directly on target. *Le Sang d'un poète* in essence is a film in which the sexual, the surrealistic, and the symbolic offer endless possibilities of exegesis, but above all it is Cocteau's personal poetic message: the beating heart of the artist in episode 1 of the film is Cocteau's. Historically, *Le Sang d'un poète* would become a landmark in the international history of the art film, a curiously shaped diamond indeed, and would run for approximately twenty years in the same theater in New York, a fact of which Cocteau would later boast in interviews dealing with the work. This film on the role of an artist in quest of self and the concomitant regenerative powers of creativity would be the first panel of a triptych in self-portrait style, juxtaposed with *Orphée* in 1950 and *Le Testament d'Orphée* in 1960. Marguerite Duras's Indian "trilogy" and Marcel Pagnol's Old Port triptych would not be too far behind.

An artistic chameleon, the versatile Cocteau could colorfully modulate his aesthetic activities from one form of expression to another, from one moment to the next. One day it would be poetry, another the novel, with a return to verse, and then a simultaneous immersion in theater and ballet. Steegmuller's image of Cocteau as a quick-change artist, a "Fregoli," captures the diversity of the talents in the poet. For more than a decade after completing *Le Sang d'un poète*, Cocteau concentrated on the stage, dipping his pen into legend and mythology with infinite possibilities of reinterpretation: *La Machine infernale* (1934), an Oedipus revisited; *Les Chevaliers de la table ronde* (1937), the acting debut of Jean Marais; *Les Parents terribles* (1938), a cause célèbre for the censors and rightists; and *Le Bel Indifférent* (1940), a play especially written for Edith Piaf and Paul Meurisse.

Sandwiched in between the patriotic newsreels and the "escape" films of World War II (1939-45) would be Cocteau's artistic contributions. Gradually the poet/playwright would be lured from the wings of the stage to the labyrinth of a film studio, but the evolution would come via the pen. For Marcel L'Herbier's *La Comédie du bonheur* (1942) with

Michel Simon, Cocteau was responsible for the adaptation from Nicolas Evreïnof's play as well as the dialogues. The following year Cocteau wrote the dialogues for the Caligarian *Baron fantôme* of Serge de Poligny and the scenario for Delannoy's *L'Eternel Retour*. The latter film, for which the poet provided *surveillance amicale*, would be a modernization of the Tristan and Isolde legend in a Gallic and Nietzschean tone, in which the couple, frustrated by love, die side by side. For Robert Bresson, Cocteau considered himself as *serviteur amical* in writing the dialogue of *Les Dames du Bois de Boulogne*, based on an episode from Diderot's *Jacques le fataliste*.

When the Italian neorealists such as Rossellini and De Sica were capturing "truth" in the postwar streets of Rome, Cocteau in 1946 busied himself in preparing an adaptation of Mme Leprince de Beaumont's charming tale of *Beauty and the Beast* written in 1757. For Cocteau, it would be a fairy tale without fairies. The film begins with the poet's invitation into the world of childhood, with his enchanting "Open Sesame!"[9] Cocteau, concerned that grown-ups never appreciate the depth of such mysteries, advises them in the preface of the film to become childlike. The narrative recounts how Belle, reminiscent of Snow White and Cinderella—kindness personified—becomes the object of the humanoid Bête's passionate love. Her sympathy for the suffering Bête breaks the spell. He is transformed into Prince Charming and marries Belle, after which, of course, the couple live happily ever after.

In this cinematic fantasy the director constructs a threefold world: The real (the house of the merchant, Belle's father), the imaginary (the chateau of Bête, filmed in the park of Raray near Senlis), and another that is semireal, semiimaginary (the pavilion of Diane). At the same time the elaborate sets of Christian Bérard, carefully designed in the style of Vermeer and Rembrandt, create another aesthetic ambiance in which this metamorphosis through love takes place. The daily trial of five hours of makeup for Jean Marais (Bête), the difficulty of getting sheets without holes for the laundry scene given the wartime exigencies, and the illness of the crew provided challenges that the inventive Cocteau soon overcame with assistance from René Clément who had just completed the Resistance film, *La Bataille du rail*.

Refashioning the theme of the suicide of the hero to discover himself and his destiny in *Le Sang d'un poète*, Cocteau designed a ballet in 1946 entitled *Le Jeune Homme et la Mort*. The "mimodrame" has been recently recast in a short color film by Roland Petit with Rudolf Nureyev assuming the role of the youth. Death, a beautiful woman elegantly dressed in black, enters the hero's room to claim her prey. The young man embarks upon an initial and final relationship with his mysterious visitor.

After she destroys the apartment, the visitor attaches a noose to a pillar/gallows, which the youth accepts as an invitation to death, and hangs himself.

The filming of *L'Aigle à deux têtes (1946), "un film théâtral,"*[10] draws us into the polemic of filmed theater and the crisis of the 1930s with Sacha Guitry and Marcel Pagnol. First staged at the Théâtre Hébertot, *L'Aigle* soon made its way to the screen with Jean Marais as the anarchist Stanislas and Edwige Feuillère as the queen. The film is a collage of images of various queens (Alexandra, Victoria, and Elizabeth of Austria). It reveals Stanislas entering the widow-queen's chamber in order to assassinate her, which would not be a loss for her, since she has abandoned all interest in life. The amorous relationship that develops in the next three days of entrapment prevents him from fulfilling his mission. Frustrated, they find that Death has the solution: Stanislas poisons himself with the queen's potion and then stabs the royal woman in his last few moments of anguish. Although not a landmark in cinema, the film, its author observed, still managed to shock a roomful of princes and ambassadors, putting them ill at ease with the controversial subject.

The exotic *Ruy Blas* of Victor Hugo found its way into Cocteau's film repertoire in 1947 with Jean Marais in the lead role. The director of the film, Pierre Billon, would cleverly utilize the scenario and dialogues prepared by the poet. The blend of the El Greco and Goya atmosphere helped evoke an imaginary Spain of the Romantic period, and the cloak-and-dagger and western elements added to the action of the film, with Marais sparkling in full acrobatic form. Cocteau considered the film more a game than anything else, and his heart was never in the production.

The next two years of Cocteau's film career (1948-50) would mark an apogee of his artistic genius. His literary works, more popular than ever, were chosen for the basis of the films of diverse directors. Roberto Rossellini, his cinematic laurels still fresh from the 1946 Cannes Festival where he was internationally acclaimed for the neorealist work *Open City*, undertook an adaptation of Cocteau's *La Voix humaine* as the first episode of his *L'Amore*. For André Zwoboda's *Les Noces de sable* inspired by a Moroccan legend, Cocteau wrote the commentary that he read in the film. Luciano Emmer had the poet compose the commentary for the short film *La Légende de Sainte Ursule*. Finally, Cocteau's own play/film *Les Parents terribles*, which stands out in this great flurry of cinematic production, is one of the works touching upon the delicate subject of incest.

The name of Oedipus has religiously been on the lips of tragedians, musicians, artists, poets, filmmakers, and psychologists for almost twenty-five centuries. Since the poet's 1926 opera-oratorio version of *Oedipus Rex* for Stravinsky (a program noted for the music of the Russian composer and the masks of the French artist), Oedipus has surfaced in Cocteau's works for almost three decades.

In 1948, dipping into his storehouse of theater pieces for ideas old and new, Cocteau decided to bring to the screen the controversial Oedipal subject of *Les Parents terribles*. The exclusive love of the mother (Yvonne) for her son (Michel) forces the father (Georges) to take a mistress (Patrice). Unfortunately, Patrice happens to be the beloved of Michel. Learning of the son's romance, the mother through jealousy and the father through anxiety attempt to disrupt the liaison between the young lovers. Yvonne in desperation commits suicide with an overdose of pills.

Playing upon the title of Tennessee Williams's *A Streetcar Named Desire,* Claude Beylie refers to the film as "une roulotte nommée délire." [11] Here order and disorder, purity and impurity, and youth and adult create the tension that climaxes in the suicide, the elimination of one of the poles of anguish.

Jean Marais, by 1948 already a very permanent fixture in Cocteau's theater and cinema repertoire, filled the role of the entrapped Michel, although playing the frisky and juvenile part long after it was suitable for him. Almost thirty years later, still dwelling under the star of Cocteau, the silver-haired thespian successfully evolved into the character of the father Georges in his own staging of *Les Parents terribles* at the Théâtre Antoine in the spring of 1977. In the program notes for this production, André Fraigneau compared Michel to a candid young Oedipus, an involuntary murderer, whereas he considered Yvonne an anarchistic Jocasta, and Georges another Creon, searching for order. The classical obsession of Cocteau shows through in his version of a *huis clos*, a perilous venture for the epoch, the poet once reflected. One can detect in the 1948 film some similarity to Louis Malle's more recent *Souffle au coeur*, wherein the theme of incest raised many an eyebrow among the cinema audiences and evoked a statement of inauthenticity from the mother of the director. Bernardo Bertolucci in *La Luna* would be just as daring with the topic.

Although filmed with a minimum of sets, the screen version of *Les Parents terribles* broke through the barrier of the theater, especially by careful editing and the use of the close-up. Despite the absence of long tracking or other intricate camera movements, the variety of shots offered the illusion of constant motion. The evolution from stage to screen thus succeeded, creating what Cocteau considered an example of the "naturalist" expression, avoiding the term *realist* since he claimed never to have known such a type of family. His primary intention to "déthéâtrer" the play was achieved, the exact opposite of the effect that he attempted with "staging" in three sweeping movements the action of *L'Aigle à deux têtes.*[12]

Twenty years after its completion, *Le Sang d'un poète* was resurrected in the recurrent themes of two films in 1950—Jean-Pierre Melville's *Les Enfants terribles* written by Cocteau in 1929, and the poet's *Orphée* first conceived by him as a play in 1925.[13] With *Les Enfants terribles* we return to the problematic world of adolescence in the Lycée Condorcet (Passage du Havre and rue d'Amsterdam). A snowball fight develops in the Cité Monthiers and the young Paul is gravely wounded with a snowball covering a rock cast by the angelic/diabolic Dargelos. Paul's friend Gérard assists him in his convalescence. Later, in the enclosed chamber of these *enfants terribles*—a sacred temple where Elisabeth is high priestess—complex relationships evolve and psychologically stifle the assembled worshippers. The brother-sister liaison of Paul and Elisabeth intensifies, disrupting the natural course of events in the budding rapport of Elisabeth with Gérard and Paul with Agathe. Paul's untimely death by poison sent by Dargelos triggers the suicide of his sister. The circle is closed.

It is not difficult to trace the sources of *Les Enfants terribles.* In general, the narrative has its origin in the Jean and Jeanne Bourgoint relationship in the 1920s. Eventually Jeanne committed suicide one Christmas Eve. The saddened and repentant Jean, after spending time at the monastery of Cîteaux, went to work with lepers in Africa where he died in 1966. For the specific characterization of Elisabeth, Cocteau had in mind Greta Garbo. Dargelos was the king of the roost at the Lycée Condorcet when Cocteau was a pupil there. Furthermore, the sepulchral atmosphere of death and suicide was occasioned by Cocteau's years of anguish following the suicide of the young Raymond Radiguet (*Le Diable au corps, Le Bal du comte d'Orgel*) in 1923.

Melville, the director of the film, specifies how the screen version originated:

> Like all the pupils of the Lycée Condorcet, I took part in those snowball fights in the Cité Monthiers, and we had all read *Les Enfants Terribles.* We considered it our book. But although I was very fond of the novel, the idea of making a film of it never entered my mind.
>
> Cocteau was a very cunning man. When he telephoned me the day after he saw *Le Silence de la Mer* to tell me he wanted me to film *Les Enfants Terribles*, he was not completely disinterested, as I might have thought at first... his admiration was sincere, but he also wanted to use me as a springboard for launching his new discovery, Edouard Dhermite [*sic*], whom he hoped to turn into another Jean Marais.[14]

In Melville's production the action becomes timeless although the cinéaste originally wanted to keep it in 1925. Cocteau complained that Christian Bérard's death left him without the genius necessary to recreate authentic sets and Melville acquiesced. The famous snowball scene of the novel, depicted very symbolically in *Le Sang d'un poète*, is reproduced in the film but without its earlier imaginative force. From the outset Cocteau was displeased with the filming. His interference on the set caused hostile feelings in Melville, and their relationship suffered thereafter.

Orphée, the second panel of the poet's classical triptych, was an amazing success, which was crowned at Cannes in 1950. As in *Le Sang*, the poet must still die in the quest for self-fulfillment in order to be reborn. In *Orphée*, Cocteau contemporizes the myth of the poet Orpheus who descends into the nether world to recover his wife Eurydice, mortally stricken by a serpent.[15] Here we have two views of the poet: the nationally established Orphée (Jean Marais) and the young, avant-garde Cégeste (Edouard Dermit). At the Café des Poètes, the Princess (Maria Casarès) claims by death the young poet Cégeste (canonized by Cocteau and fashioned in the spirit of a budding James Dean, the rebel without a cause) and later Orphée's wife. In his ambiguous manner, Cocteau insists that the Princess is not Death. In the meantime, Orphée is more concerned about the recording of a radio poetry transmission than about the safety of his wife. After Orphée's second return through the zone, the Princess, in a selfless gesture, casts the national poet back into the "dirty water" of reality to assume a renewed relationship of love with his expectant wife.

Cocteau, paving the way for Duras's evolution with *Des Journées entières dans les arbres* through the novel, play, and film, conceived of the germinal idea of *Orphée* with the angel Heurtebise in a 1925 poem, developed it in the Orphic myth in his 1926 dramatic piece, and then shaped it into a cinematic poem in 1950. Cocteau remarked that what he did with *Le Sang d'un poète* was to play an instrument clumsily with one finger, but with *Orphée* he would play with an entire orchestra. The film is an elaborate undertaking that the director insists has neither symbol nor thesis, despite its being bathed in myth and the supernatural. The bombed-out military site of Saint-Cyr shrouded in shadows, served as the zone between the two worlds of the real and the unreal. This zone would be a no-man's-land, a type of coma, according to Cocteau, constructed from human memories.[16] In the film, Cocteau himself is fragmented in the trinity of the angelic Heurtebise, the waning Orphée, desiring finally to remain an avant-garde Cégeste. Like all artists, the poet Cocteau/Orphée must appear before the tribunal of the public by which he is judged, for better or for worse.

In the same year as *Orphée* and *Les Enfants terribles*, the director made *Coriolan*, a short sixteen mm film without significance. Shot on two Sundays in the country with a few friends (Jean Marais and Josette Day), the film was organized around the subject of an eagle hunt in the thirteenth century, with Cocteau as the hunter. The filmmaker calls it a "joujou tragique," an unfortunate toy that he hoped his patronizing friend Henri Filipacchi would not parade before ciné-clubs, and the like.

In the course of the 1950s there again appeared an interest in adapting Cocteau's works; many of the resulting films, however, would be of little lasting value. The popular and popularizing poet would always be willing to provide a scenario or a commentary for an upcoming film, as in the case of *La Couronne noire* (scenario) and *Le Rouge est mis* (commentary). In 1952, with the assistance of Frédéric Rossif (*Mourir à Madrid,* 1962), Cocteau filmed his frescoes at the villa of his patron Mme Weisweiller in Saint-Jean-Cap-Ferrat. The rarely screened *Villa Santo-Sospir* in sixteen mm was televised in France in August 1973.

In 1960, already a septuagenarian and still a poet to the core, Cocteau, for the last time on film, mused over his role as poet. *Le Testament d'Orphée* would be the third and final panel of the Orphic triptych, the "summa cinematographica" of the cinéaste. Gathering together some of the cast of *Orphée* (Edouard Dermit, Jean Marais, Maria Casarès, and François Périer) and other celebrated comrades including Yul Brynner, Lucia Bose, Pablo Picasso, Charles Aznavour, and Luis-Miguel Dominguin, Cocteau filmed this epic résumé of his life and works on location in the eerie Baux de Provence and in a Nice studio in September and October, 1959. With this project Cocteau became the "Renaissance man" of cinema. He wrote the script and the dialogue, designed the elaborate masks and neoclassical costumes, and then directed and starred in the production. For technical assistance Cocteau turned to Claude Pinoteau. The film only came about through the generosity of François Truffaut who offered the backing for Cocteau's endeavor from the receipts of his celebrated Nouvelle Vague film, *Les 400 Coups*.

This self-portrait of Cocteau, via an Orphic initiation, would be his swan song. Three years before his actual death, Cocteau, the poet, "dies" in the film. In the arms of a welcoming Destiny he becomes truly himself, a veritable immortalized poet. Before he accepts Death's invitation, he is obliged to pass before the tribunal. His judges, notably *la princesse*, interrogate him about his career as a poet and filmmaker. When the princess asks him what he means by "film," he cleverly plays on words saying that a film is a "pétrifiante source de la pensée," a petrifying source of thought that revives our past actions and makes the unreal appear real.[17] On the subject of his vocation, Cocteau continued, saying that the poet uses a language that is neither living nor dead, which only a few people speak or understand. In his subtle defense Cocteau shrewdly refutes his accusers.

Following Cocteau's "death," his supernumerary friends assemble to render homage to the dead poet, but he is suddenly resurrected, a clever parallel to the reassembled hibiscus. *Le Testament* is imbued with classical myth and literary motifs. Cégeste serves as Cocteau's guide in the nether world, just as Vergil directed Dante in *The Divine Comedy*. Fittingly, Yul Brynner announces, "Abandon all hope ye who enter here." As Cégeste and Cocteau continue on their promenade, they pass Antigone assisting the blind Oedipus, a flashback to the poet's preoccupation with the mythical figure. This defense and illustration of Cocteau's calling as a poet is preserved on celluloid, his own last will and testament. Francis Steegmuller, however, would not be pleased with the results, referring to Cocteau's finale in cinema as "the mawkish *Testament d'Orphée,* a regrettable item in his film legacy."[18]

Once Cocteau took up the camera he assumed the role of a sorcerer's apprentice. With a clever legerdemain he would put the spectator in the hypnotic state of a collective, wakening dream, and, à la Méliès, would unfold mysteries of another dimension. The film viewer who penetrates into Cocteau's personal cinematic zone must follow Yul Brynner's counsel and "abandon all hope," that is, all hope of understanding, naturally, as the viewer was just beginning to do with the Robbe-Grillet, Resnais, or Duras films in the early 1960s. Instead, the film enthusiast must be prepared to *feel* and to *believe.*

At Cocteau's first entrance into the "dream factory," the poet felt he was trespassing and would be received by the established cinéastes as warmly as a dog wandering through a game of tenpins, to use his imagery. His presentiment was accurate. Jean Cocteau was always fascinated by the force of the visual image, often describing it as a powerful weapon in the hands of a poet. For Cocteau, it was a young art, and he, above all, was chronically in love with youth. In 1946, he already sensed that this budding medium would soon acquire for itself a title of nobility, and referred to this tenth Muse as "écriture de demain," the writing of tomorrow on which Marshall McLuhan would wax eloquently in his prophetic moments. Cocteau differed from the North American oracle who, in convoluted terms, sounded the death knell for literature. In the poet's eyes, literature would not have to die before cinema could mature as an art, but instead the two Muses could sing and dance in blissful harmony, perhaps, one might say, as if in a Botticelli tableau.

For Cocteau, the cinema would primarily be a vehicle for his poetry. A "poète maudit"[19] in the lineage of a Villon, Baudelaire, Verlaine, or Rimbaud, Cocteau did not *follow* the norms of society, of literature, or of cinema, but instead *created* them. Through his divine calling he made of poetry a sacred temple wherein he plays high priest and in which the first commandment is "to thine own self be true!" Pursuing the same theme he would use in *Le Testament d'Orphée*, Cocteau shed some light on this vocation in his address at the Académie française:

> Poets are only slaves of a power which resides deep within them, slaves of a master who uses them but whose face they do not recognize, the face which perhaps may be their own.[20]

A supple instrument in the hands of Destiny, Cocteau resembles Orphée listening attentively to the cryptic message—R.R.7.2.3.7.3.5.5.7.12 or "The bird sings with its fingers." The poetic transmission on the car radio comes from beyond. The poet's mission will be to reveal this discovery of transcendental "truth" to the public and in so doing become immortal.

Just as Cocteau the cinéaste used the camera to permit others to dream, he utilized his poets (Orphée, Cégeste, himself, and all his angelic heroes) as his message bearers. They are the *demi-dieux* who serve as intermediaries with the ability to pierce the barrier beyond which lie the mysteries of the universe. The blessed poet must instinctively follow his vocation to die in order to be reborn, making a place for his works while establishing himself as immortal. The young artist in *Le Sang*, Cégeste and Orphée in *Orphée,* and Cocteau in *Le Testament* pass through the portal of death to encounter the sacred truths of another world. By the tribunal in *Le Testament*, Cocteau is acused of fraudulently penetrating a world that is not his. He admits his deed and claims to have deliberately attempted to leap over the mysterious fourth wall upon which men write their loves and dreams.[21] His intention to communicate with this hermetic domain may not always be actualized. Neal Oxenhandler describes Cocteau's confrontation with this universe:

> The whole universe is mysterious, and Cocteau retreats, finally to a kind of resigned skepticism. Perhaps the Mystery cannot be explained at all; his mystery as an individual is inherent in the greater Mystery of the universe. "The mistake must have been to try to understand what goes on in every storey of the building."[22]

When Cocteau nodded playfully in the direction of Descartes with his "I dream, therefore I am," he professed his faith in another dimension of Life/Death's kingdom into which he will ingeniously seduce the spectator. The unreal/real zone is a brief glimpse into the beyond, an unsettling region of the poet's imagination. *Le Sang d'un poète* would be a "realistic documentary of unreal events," where dream and reality flow gently in the same stream. To recreate graphically this "other world," Cocteau inserts into his films the play of mirrors that serve as irrefutable signs of our aging, but more so as the threshold to the beyond. In his construction of duplicate rooms separated by the framework of a mirror, an optical illusion is produced, just as with the 400 kilogram mercury tub in *Orphée*.

Cocteau's magical skills further abound as he continues to blend the natural with the supernatural: human hands emerge from the wall bearing the candelabra in *La Belle et la bête*, flowers bud quickly or disappear, and gloves have the power to allow entry into the new dimension. Cocteau passes an image of himself in *Le Testament* and cleverly dies with a javelin piercing his body. Chance would have it that as the javelin was cast a jet plane streaked through the sky with a shrieking sound. The noise served as a perfect sound effect in the scene. Méliès lives on in Cocteau, but the poet goes one step beyond the pioneer filmmaker in constructing a philosophy of illusion.

Love and death—the two major themes found in any respectable poet's repertoire—are intricately linked in Cocteau's films. Once in love, the poet finds himself tragically unfulfilled because of some forces outside of him, by limits set through societal norms. *La Belle et la bête* reflects a sympathetic, sacrificial love of Belle for the sensitive monster Bête. This irregular love triumphs when Bête is transformed into the handsome Avenant, and the latter becomes the corpse of Bête. Patrice, the beloved of Michel in *Les Parents terribles*, discovers herself caught in a web encircling the Oedipal love of the mother and son (a precursor of Duras's mother/son relationship in *Des Journées entières dans les arbres*) and the illicit love of Michel's father Georges. These *parents terribles* serve as disconcerting examples of adults who generate the *enfants terribles* and their resulting incestuous love. In both cases, the enclosure of the room reinforces the stifling atmosphere of an abnormal love. *Orphée* is a cinematic circle of love: The princess loves Orphée, Heurtebise loves Eurydice, whereas Orphée only loves his own image and his poetry. In a selfless gesture, *la princesse* allows Orphée to piece together the shambles of his love relationship with his wife Eurydice. The queen of *L'Aigle à deux têtes* is resurrected through the rapport with the anarchist Stanislas only to die three days later. For Stanislas there is no other means than death to escape the dilemma of love and *engagement*.

Love restricted in human relations finds fulfillment only through death. For the poet, death is the climax of creativity and love, the means toward the end, his immortality. The specter of death, nonetheless, traveled by Cocteau's side throughout his life, perhaps coloring his vision of life and love, from the death of his father in 1899 to the war victims that he had known, but most important to his friends Raymond Radiguet, Roland Garros, and Jeanne Bourgoint. In the second episode of *Le Sang*, the artist commits suicide and is crowned with laurels in the final segment of the film. The Princess of *Orphée* in her Rolls-Royce is an instrument of death or perhaps death itself, escorted by her motorcycle aides inspired by General Giraud's funeral cortège. Very elegantly dressed, she dominates the scene, directing her aides to carry out the plans of destiny. The Princess was Christian Bérard's conception, although Cocteau already sketched out this character in germinal form in *Le Jeune Homme et la Mort* (1946). Suicide in *L'Aigle* resolves the tension of philosophical and passionate penchants. The simultaneous death by poison and stabbing may appear a bit theatrical, but it nevertheless follows a pattern of frustrated love scenes in Cocteau's opus. In *Les Parents terribles*, the suicide of Yvonne eliminates one of the psychological and physical powers that restrains Michel from pursuing his love of Patrice. Like *L'Aigle, Les Enfants terribles* terminates on a note of double death. Paul poisons himself and his sister Elisabeth puts a revolver to her head. In dying, Bête becomes Prince Charming, one of the few "happy endings" that Cocteau filmed. But in most fairy tales are not the hero and the heroine normally destined to live happily ever after? Death, for the artist with a vocation as poet, is an absolutely necessary ingredient in life, Cocteau insists. The poet must pass through a series of successive deaths in order to become fully himself.[23] Although death in all its manifestations holds the trump cards in Cocteau's cinematic schema of things, the artist ideally emerges the victor.

André Maurois designated Cocteau a mythmaker, and that he was. Keeping company with Sartre (*Les Mouches*), Anouilh (*Antigone*), and Giraudoux (*La Guerre de Troie n'aura pas lieu*), Cocteau utilized classical myths to heighten the awareness in a contemporary public of a theme in antiquity that recurs throughout man's history. In the past, audiences could not but recognize their problems, moments of anguish, or political struggles in another drama of yesterday, just as French Resistants and Fascists alike saw themselves mirrored in the characters of Antigone and Creon.

Cocteau's treatment of myth is subservient to a narcissistic ideology of the poet struggling with the forces of love and death. At the same time, he transforms the myth, embellishes it, and refracts it in multiple ways in his films. The spectator who witnesses the unfolding of the filmed narrative of antiquity resembles the Athenian of the Golden Age intently watching an author's unique treatment of a familiar myth. Since the early 1920s Cocteau became involved with the Sphinx, Bacchus, Orpheus, Oedipus, and Antigone, in each situation disclosing his personal interpretation of the myth. Discussing his constant use of the personage of Orpheus in his theater and cinema, the poet remarked that he identified with the poet of antiquity insofar as he himself limps with one foot in this life and the other in death.[24] Cocteau, committed to the two worlds, in a free,

Dionysian spirit plays in and reveals the secrets of both, in a well-organized, structured, Apollonian framework of films like *Le Sang d'un poète* and *Orphée*.

During the tribunal scene in *Le Testament*, Cégeste inquires of Cocteau if he is the expert in phoenixology.[25] The aging poet of course admits his obsession with the theme. Writing about this subject he observes: "The spirit stirs, chafes at its bonds, exults, burns and rises again from the ashes. This stationary motion ought to be studied and the new science might well be called phoenixology."[26] Such a notion of death and resurrection is at the core of Christian and Greek mythology, and dovetails perfectly in Cocteau's thematic presentation of the poet's immortality achieved only through death.

The same sense of myth pervades the other realms of Cocteau's works. *Renaud et Armide*, the tales of *Les Chevaliers de la table ronde*, and the fairy tale of *La Belle et la bête* are used by the playwright/cinéaste as a "véritable mythologie française."[27] The collaboration of Cocteau and Delannoy in *L'Eternel Retour* resulted in an eerie portrait in relief of a modern Tristan and Isolde, a film whose overtones are simultaneously Gallic, Norman, Germanic, and Scandinavian.

Cocteau in his eight principal films has left his imprint upon the history of cinema. His is a universe pervaded by the unreal and ethereal, although the poet claims that it is real. This realm is one of evasion, imbued with mystery, situated beyond all laws. Inhabiting it are the poets and the nonpoets, the former obviously being the heroes. All action and interaction have their origin in the interior and exterior struggles of these poets against a society that prevents them from being true to their respective natures. A personal, somewhat Platonic ideal forms the major preoccupation of the poets, and their entire lives are spent in quest of it. What is this ideal if not the absolute purity of each, *l'angélisme*? Bordering on the genius, they strive toward this goal of being noncommitted, self-centered, and rebellious, and suffer persecution for the sake of their individualism. These poets are the demigods who experience total freedom or seek to attain it, and in some way control life and death. The heroes differ from the other members of society by their attempts to know the meaning of life and their own personal natures, and possessing Cocteau's nonconformist spirit of courage, they take their destiny in their own hands.

Cocteau almost always moved against the current, perhaps in a type of permanent avant-garde. He says he passed through many isms, but we can see that he was never fully attracted by any one of them. The poet/cinéaste would be noted for his fruitful collaboration with other artists, notably musicians like Auric and Stravinsky, and painters like Picasso and Dufy. His neoclassical sets showed originality whereas his avant-garde film techniques paved the way for experimental films, which were obvious in the area of special effects. Cocteau's poetic spirit would predominate in all his contributions to film, and in the final analysis, this cinéaste would resemble a gossamerlike substance that catches everything including the light, but is not caught itself. When touched it vanishes.

Cocteau: *Le Sang d'un poète,* **1930.**

Cocteau: *L'Eternel Retour,* **1943.**

Cocteau: *La Belle et la bête,* **1946.**

Cocteau: *La Belle et la bête,* **1946.**

Billon/Cocteau: *Ruy Blas,* **1946.**

Cocteau: *L'Aigle à deux têtes*, **1947.**

Cocteau: *L'Aigle à deux têtes*, **1947.**

Cocteau: *Les Parents terribles*, **1948.**

Cocteau: *Les Parents terribles*, **1948.**

Cocteau: *Orphée*, **1950.**

Cocteau: *Orphée,* **1950.**

Cocteau: ***Orphée,*** **1950.**

Melville/Cocteau: *Les Enfants terribles,* **1950.**

Melville/Cocteau: *Les Enfants terribles,* **1950.**

2

SACHA GUITRY

To chase after documents and to vow never to commit any mistake voluntarily... To verify the names and control the dates, To have only one dream: to entertain like an acrobat, promising onself never to lie.

—*Remontons les Champs-Elysées (1938)*

To utter the name of Sacha Guitry in the French cinema world opens the floodgates to a wave of spontaneous reactions, not all of which are favorable. Guitry has often been compared with Cocteau as a jack-of-all-trades (but still a genius) and with Pagnol as a fabricator of *théatre de conserve*, perhaps affectionately translated as "theater in a tin can," or "canned drama," since he primarily filmed many works initially intended for the stage. The filmmakers of his day would have preferred specialization in one medium or another, and a boulevardier taking up a camera would not have been taken seriously. Some critics have linked Guitry with the Cecil B. de Mille exotic productions whereas others have been all too quick to cast in his face the label "collaborator." Guitry has thus been condemned to purgatory in the history of French cinema. In the heat of the polemic it is all too easy to forget Guitry's contribution to the cultural milieu of the Paris stage as well as to world cinema. His career as the relentless genius of the boulevard theater may have on occasion dissolved to simple film entertainer of "tout Paris," when Paris was yesterday,[1] as Janet Flanner describes it, but let us try to determine his true place in historical perspective.

Sacha Guitry's past was rooted in the theater. He was born in Russia in 1885 in what was then Saint Petersburg and is now Leningrad. At the time of his birth, his father Lucien, an accomplished actor, was on his annual tour of Russia; the precocious lad soon found himself on stage before children his age were making their way to school for the first time. At the age of five he played for Alexander III of Russia; at fourteen he was before the footlights at Versailles; at seventeen he penned his first play; at nineteen he was involved in his first professional role at the Théâtre de la Renaissance; and at the age of thirty he made his first film. The list of early "firsts" is impressive. At a young age he was already well established in the arts, but it would only be the beginning; a novel, poetry, and essays would soon follow. If anything, Guitry was one of the most prolific artists of his generation. At his death in 1957, he left a heritage of 120 plays and twenty-six films—a vast repertoire of works punctuated by isolated masterpieces.

Guitry's cinematic projects in general mirror a significant part of his theatrical production. A more detailed pattern that can be detected from these numerous films, however, reflects four modes or phases in his lengthy career. The first is Guitry's rite of passage into the cinema world during the height of the silent film epoch. The second stage entails the filming of his own plays, which manifests a light, boulevard style. The third phase is the historical and biographical film usually imbued with fantasy. Finally, his career terminated on a more somber note, with the last few films bearing the mark of a sickly man scarred by society.

On 23 November 1915, at the Parisian Théâtre des Variétés, Guitry projected for his captive, wartime audience what may have been a prophecy of the future of cinema—a "talkie" *avant la lettre*. It was still the era of the silent film, the same year that Griffith released his monumental *Birth of a Nation*, and more than a decade before the sound revolution in film. In the spirit of nationalism and as a response to the Germans who were so boastful of their culture, Guitry gathered together for a film, *Ceux de chez nous*, the cream of France's artists and politicians, friends of his father Lucien Guitry. He filmed the septuagenarian Sarah Bernhardt; then Anatole France writing and arranging his books; Auguste Rodin chipping away at a block of marble in his studio; Camille Saint-Saëns directing an orchestra; Edmond Rostand composing a sonnet; Auguste Renoir semiparalyzed, before his easel, being supported by his son Jean; Claude Monet painting near his famous lily pond; and the reluctant Edgar Degas caught off guard, strolling in the street. The images of these celebrities would be engraved on celluloid and left for posterity. Besides the close-up portrait effect utilized by Guitry, the most striking part of the presentation of *Ceux de chez nous* in 1915 was the "speech" of these characters. As the image was projected on the screen, Guitry and his wife Charlotte Lysès, speaking from backstage, put words into their mouths, synchronizing the sound with the lip movements of the figures on the screen. The audience at the Théâtre des Variétés was participating in a historical moment but did not realize it.

Following this debut in the film world as director (although very nonprofessional), Guitry, well at ease in the spotlights, next tried his theatrical skills before the camera. In the film *Un Roman d'amour et d'aventures* (1918), directed by René Hervil and Louis Mercanton, Guitry played the roles of two brothers, Jean Sarrazin, director of an industrial bank, and his look-alike brother Jacques, a literary character. Yvonne Printemps, Guitry's second wife, took the part of Ketty. The double characterization will recur in Michel Simon's portrayal of the Ménard-Lacoste brothers in *La Vie d'un honnête homme* (1952), one of the several fascinating, collaborative endeavors of Simon and Guitry.

Concentrating on the stage, the "last of the boulevardiers" was still not committed to cinema during the late 1920s and early 1930s. Directors from America and England, as well as France, began to adapt the playwright's theater for the screen. The American director Harry Beaumont transposed Guitry's stage production about the nineteenth century French mime Jean-Gaspard Debureau, entitling the film *The Lover of Camille* (1924). Seymour Hicks, a British filmmaker, adapted Guitry's play *Faisons un rêve* for the film *Sleeping Partners* (1930). His stage works thus gained an international audience, while on the home scene in 1935, Léonce Perret filmed *Les Deux Couverts*, which Guitry had written twenty years earlier.

In 1929, Guitry still did not seem very enamored of the cinema. Looking at the other side of the Atlantic where sound film was becoming a commonplace following Al Jolson's performance in *The Jazz Singer* (1927), Guitry felt that the "talkies" would harm the cinema but would be beneficial for the theater.[2] Film, in Guitry's mind, had reached its apogee with Chaplin, whose praises he would sing well into the sound era.

The wooing process of the experienced dramatist by the universe of the motion picture was gradual. In 1931, Guitry allowed the producers Pierre Braunberger and Roger Richebé to adapt his play *Le Blanc et le noir*. Robert Florey, assisted by Gide's protégé Marc Allégret, assumed the responsibility of the direction of the film, casting for the work two actors who shortly would become associated with Marcel Pagnol—Fernandel and Raimu. Sound still was a novel adventure for the French filmmakers, with Pagnol in the avant-garde. Guitry's public would now be further enlarged to international dimensions, and his plays were easily transposed for the screen by force of their structure and length.

Twenty years after his debut with *Ceux de chez nous*, Guitry was finally seduced into making his own films. He accepted the responsibility for filming two works in 1935—*Pasteur* and *Bonne Chance*, which mark the next phase of his evolution in converting his own stage material for the screen. In such works, often light comedies, Guitry would treat in boulevard style the themes of love, happiness, and humor, which is obvious in two of his other works of 1937 vintage—*Désiré* and *Quadrille.* Once at ease on both sides of the camera, for the next twenty years Guitry would film many of his works and at the same time guard the lead role for himself, just as he did on stage. He thus came about-face since 1929 in his sentiments for film. Now he would show great devotion to this medium, which disseminated his own image twenty-four times a second. In 1931, solidly entrenched in this new world of art, Guitry admitted in an interview that he was definitely enamored of the cinema.[3]

François Mars in his article "Citizen Sacha" was not opposed to Guitry's use of the genre of *théâtre filmé* as a vehicle of expression. Yet with a slight bit of disdain, Mars put into this category of filmed theater such works as *The Ten Commandments, The Bridge on the River Kwai*, and Clément/Duras's *This Angry Age.*[4]

Guitry's intimate manner of speaking of love and later his sarcasm about the vicissitudes of life reflect the gamut of his abilities to utilize the content of his theater pieces and to embroider them with fresh cinematic possibilities. In *Désire,* however, he retained his theatrical approach to the material by addressing the public and then paging through a photograph album containing the cast. Although on occasion he would write an original script, as for *Donne-moi tes yeux* and *La Malibran*—both filmed in 1943—Guitry would ordinarily exploit his own stage productions.

The war left its scars on the entertainer. Arrested at the time of the Liberation, Guitry was obliged to spend sixty days in prison. He was accused of collaborating with the enemy, that is, of being too polite to German officers and acquiring contraband material (coal to preserve his collections, he insisted). He was forced to take leave of the Académie Goncourt to which he was elected in 1939. It would be some time before he would recover from this blow, not unlike the situation of the blacklisted filmmakers during the McCarthy period in the United States. His journals document this tragic rupture in his artistic career.

Set in motion by the same fervor as the classical filmmakers Dreyer, Bresson, and Gance for re-creating past epochs as backdrops for personal dramas, Guitry often filmed historical and biographical portraits in grandiose detail. He was always fascinated by these two approaches and in the early 1950s had already recorded on film *Pasteur* and *Debureau*, as well as *Les Perles de la couronne* and *Remontons les Champs-Elysées.*

In the autumn of his life the cinéaste embarked upon yet another phase of this historical adventure. Three films are indicative of the trend in Guitry's creations: *Si Versailles m'était conté* (1953), *Napoléon* (1954), and *Si Paris nous était conté* (1955). Far from being realistic, these works manifest the cast-of-thousands approach that is so common in Cecil B. de Mille's productions, such as *The Greatest Show on Earth* and *The Ten Commandments*. These films of Guitry were constructed on magnificent sets and required precious time to cast and design, and hence were more ambitious undertakings than Guitry's previous films. A rival of Abel Gance's classic, Guitry's *Napoléon* required five months to film, which for him was a considerable investment of time.

In these historical enterprises, lavish costumes, extravagant sets, and an innumerable international cast (Eric von Stroheim, Claudette Colbert, Jean-Louis Barrault, Orson Welles, Jean-Pierre Aumont, Jean Gabin, Michèle Morgan, Danielle Darrieux, Gérard Philipe, and others) created a dazzling aura of romanticized pageantry. To those who would challenge this approach to historical events and call them distortions, Guitry would probably reply that all history is subjective. It is certainly history *as he would like to have seen it*, in all of its pomp and circumstance.

In his *Si Versailles m'était conté*, Guitry (Louis XIV) was perfectly comfortable in his royal milieu descending the large staircase followed by his regal cortège. He would henceforth be known as "le Roi de Paris." Occasionally Guitry's treatment of the historical scene is humorous, created more for amusement than for instruction, a *point de départ* for his own fantasies and anecdotes. Guitry's purpose was to entertain his public like an acrobat.[5] At other times he would use history in a moralizing fashion, for example, as he explained to a group of children their national heritage.

In these ostentatious frescoes of France's days of glory, Guitry would insert himself into the work as its principal character, incarnating a Louis XI, Louis XIV, or Talleyrand. Earlier in his films Guitry juggled several roles during the same work, for instance, in *Les Perles de la couronne* in which he assumed the parts of François I, Barras, Napoléon III, and the writer Jean Martin. This flamboyant appearance on center stage, plus his cult of publicity until his paralysis, gained for Guitry the unfortunate reputation among some critics of being a selfish and vain individual, whereas others looked upon the same situation and regarded it as a spirit of inventiveness in creating a multitude of diversified personae.

With the last few films of his career Guitry entered into a certain winter of discontent. His cinematic work was tinted by his declining health and his troubled perspective on life. Soured by his political difficulties, elderly, and sickly, he nonetheless made his way to the studio, at times in a wheelchair, or supervised the editing from his bed. Louis Marcorelles accurately describes this final phase:

> During the last few years, apart from his historical pictures, Guitry rediscovered, in *La Poison* and *Assassins et Voleurs*, an almost diabolic aptitude for describing thieves and rogues. He approached villainy with relish, deliberation and a characteristically macabre humour, hurling by the way a few darts at an immoral and cynical society. As an observer of human behaviour, he was ruthless and disillusioned, a confirmed enemy of the high-sounding, empty phrase.[6]

Guitry's personal obsession with death and darkness impregnated his later works. This vein was evident already in *La Poison* (1951), but it also continued through *Les Trois font la paire* (1957) and *La Vie à deux* (1958). Clément Duhour, who assisted the ailing Guitry in *Les Trois font la paire*, took full charge of the Guitry-scripted *La Vie à deux* and released the work after the latter's death. The king of the boulevard was always fascinated by the idea of a sketch or vignette both on stage and in film, especially since the days of *Ils étaient neuf célibataires*. In *La Vie à deux* Guitry offered four sketches of couples that can be considered "une petite anthologie du théâtre."[7] Guitry the actor almost never assumed a secondary role in his works during his creative period, but in the waning years of his professional career, he was obliged to have Michel Simon or Jean Poiret take the limelight in his stead. Guitry gracefully made his bow and left the stage.

For Guitry to have concocted his kaleidoscopic world of illusion demanded genius and energy, both of which he possessed in abundance. His method of operating was basically the same for the majority of his films. Except for his *films d'auteur* and the extravaganzas he created explicitly for the cinema, he would ordinarily adapt one of his plays, developing with humor and later with sarcasm, the themes of love, chance, happiness, and success. The 1918 play *Debureau* evolved into a film in 1950, whereas *Tu m'as sauvé la vie*, staged in 1949, was filmed the following year. During the 1940s and 1950s he wrote the dialogue for specific actors, as in the case of Fernandel (*Adhémar ou le jouet de la fatalité*). Normally the artist would cast the same actors in the cinema and theater productions. Guitry would be proud of the fact that he could film the theater piece without much difficulty in very little time, offering as an explanation the fact that actors often played the same role more than 200 times on stage before finding themselves in front of the camera.

In a manner that was very similar to Pagnol, Guitry accentuated the primacy of the text, correcting the dialogue when necessary and making incredible demands upon the cast. In certain films such as *Désiré* he would even transfer the data normally found in written form in the credits to an oral presentation. Throughout the rehearsals and filming, Guitry would continue to scribble dialogues and murmur the parts over and over to himself. Rehearsing often at very great length, he ordinarily filmed each scene but once. As principal actor, he would know his role thoroughly, having written and staged the play countless times before the filming began. Each of his wives would also enjoy a privileged part in his films, for example, Geneviève de Sereville in *Le Destin fabuleux de Désirée Clary*; Lana Marconi in *Le Diable boiteux* and *Je l'ai été trois fois*; and Jacqueline Delubac in *Le Nouveau Testament* as well as *Le Roman d'un tricheur*.

Guitry worked very deliberately with his film crew, giving them specific directions in nontechnical language and presuming their competence. He required them to be present at the rehearsals in order to get a feeling for the movement and the dialogue, observed François Gir, assistant to Pagnol and Guitry.[8] René Renoux, the set designer for the last films of Guitry, utilized many of the ideas that the cinéaste penciled on scrap paper at odd moments of his complicated working day.

The actual filming period would be very brief. *La Poison* was completed in nine days: *Le Diable boiteux* in sixteen: and *Dubureau* in twelve; but the record may be his *Mot de Cambronne*, filmed in four hours! The more elaborate works took four to five months because of the complexity of the sets, camera positions, costuming, and locations.

During the filming and editing processes, Guitry would prove himself a master of tricks in the tradition of Méliès. Both witty and inventive, he would use on occasion one of his favorite illusions—an actor playing a double role, for instance Michel Simon's dual part in *La Vie d'un honnête homme*. Although he would supervise the editing, Guitry did not involve himself in the meticulous technical tasks. He would see entire scenes projected for him on screen. He preferred viewing the work in the advanced stage of cutting and assembly, having already made most of the adjustments in the course of the filming, side by side with his editor.

In assessing Guitry's film production over four decades, the critic would be obliged to say that his work is colossal but of uneven quality. The majority of his public is attracted to either his historical pageants or his *films d'auteur*. What has Sacha Guitry in fact left as a heritage? His versatility and nimble-wittedness as expressed earlier brought about 120 dramatic pieces, some of which enjoyed lengthy runs of several months, which meant constant rehearsals and almost nightly performances. His thirty-six films were less demanding but still exacted considerable hours of preparation and studio time—especially in major productions—and a certain spirit of inventiveness. He would often say, however, that he created only for his own pleasure. Before he died in July, 1957, Guitry admitted that only one third or one half of the countless projects that he had conceived were ever realized. Judging from what has been left in the wake of this prolific artist, we can see that film was primarily for Guitry a means of preserving the freshness of a theatrical experience, as his secretary Stéphane Prince observed about "Le Maître," as he was commonly titled.[9] For example, Prince noted that Raimu died in 1948, yet he lives on in film (*Faisons un rêve* or *Le Blanc et le noir*). In the same manner the image of Guitry as actor and director is conserved via his own films and is then immortalized in a short film sketch of the cinéaste/playwright by Prince, *Le Musée Sacha Guitry* (1951).

Guitry, the undisputed master of the boulevard theater, inherited from the Belle Epoque, as Louis Marcorelles indicates, "its taste for luxury, its insolence and extravagance."[10] This spirit carried over into his film ventures, as he captured the popular mythology of each decade that he filmed. In a moralizing vein he entertained society with clever caricatures of itself, constructed from his careful observations of the foibles of mankind. Some of his materials may be dated, despite his efforts to generalize the particular situation. He would try to avoid giving specific dates and prices of articles, for example. With women's fashions, Guitry encountered much difficulty. He once remarked that he liked to have his actresses wear bérets, since women's hats could be too easily dated, whereas a béret is timeless, or so he thought.

Organized again around the theme of "Cinéma et Histoire," the annual Valence Film Festival of April 1977 included French and Italian films from the 1950s by Grémillon, Cayatte, Allégret, Duvivier, Bresson, and Rossellini. Guitry's *La Vie d'un honnête homme* with Michel Simon formed part of the program. Such films of Guitry serve today as a sociological witness to the taste and mood of a certain period and can stand on their own when compared to the vintage of films of the same epoch. The 1940s and 1950s, especially, have left their impression on Guitry's works, and he, in turn, has left his cinematic stamp on this season in our history.

Guitry: *Le Diable boiteux,* **1948.**

Guitry: *La Poison*, **1951.**

Guitry: *La Vie d'un honnête homme,* **1952.**

Guitry: *Si Versailles m'était conté*, **1953.**

3

MARCEL PAGNOL

A film for me is an object that is constantly being modified, not at all something made sacred by a certain concept of Art.

—Les Lettres Françaises (1969)

On March 1947, Marcel Pagnol in all his elegance and eloquence stood before the assembled Immortals of the Académie française and accepted the honor of being admitted to this illustrious constellation of savants. With him cinema entered the Academy (only a parenthesis in his life, according to Audouard[1]), and Jean Cocteau and René Clair would soon follow him into the Academy. On that March afternoon, under the cupola of the Academy along the Left Bank of the Seine, Pagnol, with his sword designed with a strip of celluloid at his side, proclaimed that a new art had been born, the art of cinema. (Although already a half century old, cinema in 1947 was still rarely considered an art.) With his next qualification, however, Pagnol would provoke repeated assaults from the demons of the world of criticism who would not easily be exorcised. As he had done on previous occasions, Pagnol in his speech to the Académie referred to cinema, this "theatre of shadows," as but a "minor art," unable to create the actual works, but destined to merely serve as a vehicle of the creative writings of novelists and playwrights.[2]

This comment and the "heresy" of filming plays obliged him to share the same opprobrium that was heaped upon Sacha Guitry.[3] The critics would see that the imprinting of his own or other playwright's texts on celluloid would preserve the presence and dynamism of the characters and allow for a more extensive distribution starting with Paris, gaining momentum in the provinces, and finally making its way to the other side of the Atlantic. This process of filming plays would be less costly than the task of working with larger, star-studded casts on an exotic location with massive sums of francs or dollars in the wings. In fact, the recorded play could document the epoch in a very concrete manner, for which the film historians are appreciative. The discussion of the *théâtre filmé* continued on, developing into the "cas Pagnol," which André Bazin attempted to elucidate.[4] The critics judged the action and the recitation of lines in a Pagnol film as too artificial since the work was originally designed with the limitations of the stage in mind. Fossilization often took place. The revolutionary industry of the sound film had become only the silent film with words and noises, nothing more, and the camera simply attended the play with the audience. In the early days of sound, however, the technical possibilities had not yet emerged, and Pagnol would still be restricted in this new aesthetic expression. Sharing the fate of the boulevardier Guitry and the Renoir of the "staged" film, Pagnol would thus be judged severely for his endeavors of transferring drama from stage to screen.

Like the rose of the Petit Prince, which was born at the same time as the sun, Pagnol was born at the same time as the cinema in 1895 at Aubagne, but a stone's throw from La Ciotat where the Lumière brothers were documenting the historic arrival of the train into the station. He barely missed coming into the world at La Ciotat where his mother was heading for the baby's delivery when her labor pains en route obliged her to return home. The sun and charm of the Marseilles region that was instilled in him early on in his life would never leave him. The literary-oriented Marcel would then come through the ranks of the teaching profession and inherit the instinct to communicate his wisdom from his father Joseph who taught in the local schools. Exposed to an academic world not unlike that of *Topaze* and *Merlusse*, and which was filled with gradations of rank, merits, and palms, the young Pagnol had great aspirations. His dream of teaching at the Lycée Condorcet, this "Cathedral of Learning"[5] made famous by Cocteau's *Les Enfants terribles*, came true in 1922. His days of glory at the lycée, however, would be brief. The theater world soon beckoned and he succumbed. Pagnol in the shoes of Topaze left his teaching career to launch himself in a new profession, finding a "real" challenging world outside the doors of the lycée. His stroke of genius in performing his play *Topaze* in October 1928 at the Variétés (where his predecessor Sacha Guitry had earlier experimented with sound in 1915) and then his *Marius* in March 1929 at the Théâtre de Paris, signaled Pagnol's professional entry into the world of the arts.

The year 1929, marred by financial tragedy in the United States, witnessed the sound film's sensational impact upon Europe, just two years after Al Jolson titillated the American public with *The Jazz Singer*. Pierre Blanchard, a close friend of Pagnol, had just returned from

London where Harry Beaumont and Edmund Goulding's sound motion picture *Broadway Melody* was enjoying a successful run.[6] Pagnol's curiosity was aroused, and he soon traveled to London to see for himself what this extraordinary phenomenon might be. Once back in France he would begin his pioneering activities. In the advent of the sound film, Pagnol, with the same solemnity as Nietzsche's "God is dead," prophesied the death blow to the theater as well as to the silent film. As film theoretician in an art that he called "Cinématurgie," Pagnol still had high hopes that the sound film would "reinvent the theater."[7] Already the first shots of the battle of filmed theater could be faintly heard in the distance.

The sound film was not yet fully on its feet when a Hungarian filmmaker by the name of Alexander Korda arrived in Paris from the Babylon of Hollywood. Korda would be part of an enterprising group from Paramount Studios who established what Nino Frank graphically referred to as the "Babel-sur-Seine". Capitalizing on the popularity of sound, filmmakers and businessmen alike set about filming the same work in fifteen different languages ready for export the world over. Korda was to make a sound film of Pagnol's *Marius*, the tale of a youth from Marseilles filled with wanderlust, hesitating between his beloved Fanny and the deep blue sea. Korda told Pagnol that he himself would take care of the technical aspects of the film, but that the author should assume the full responsiblity for the written text. The novelty of sound and the brilliant éclat of the play assured a name for the young playwright as well as for the actors who would later become an integral part of Pagnol's coterie: Raimu (César), Pierre Fresnay (Marius), and Orane Demazis (Fanny). *Marius* would be the dramatist's rite of initiation into the shadowy world of illusions.

Marc Allégret, the young protégé of André Gide, accompanied the established novelist to Africa in 1926 and returned to France with his first film, a short work entitled *Voyage au Congo*. After serving as assistant to Robert Florey, Allégret undertook his first feature film, *Fanny*, tapping the dramatic resources of Marcel Pagnol. In 1932, Allégret released the film resurrecting the colorful characters of the Old Port of Marseilles as described by Pagnol. Although pregnant by her seafaring Marius, Fanny decides to marry Panisse, advanced in age, in order to assure a future for the expected child. For the production of *Fanny*, Pagnol contributed the scenario and the dialogues.

In the same year as *Fanny*'s completion, Louis Gasnier filmed the first version of *Topaze*, and Roger Lion brought to the screen *Un Direct au coeur*, both emanating from Pagnol's literary repertoire. The following year, 1933, signaled a major step in Pagnol's artistic career. He first produced *L'Agonie des aigles* and, with Roger Richebé as director, adapted *Les Demisoldes* from the Georges d'Esparbès novel. *Le Gendre de Monsieur Poirier*, the first film that Pagnol personally signed, would soon bring him directly into the world of *théâtre filmé*. In September of that year he also founded Les Auteurs Associés, with his brother René and Marcel Gras as directors of production and Marcel as filmmaker, the keystone in this novel enterprise. With the assistance of Arno Brun and Gabriel d'Aubarède he initiated the *Cahiers du Film*, which served as a vehicle for his theories on film, especially the development of sound. For this journal with a circulation aimed at 5,000, Pagnol traced the genealogy of cinema and observed how the silent film would disappear and the sound film would begin to make a contribution to the arts and sciences. The film journal only lasted three issues. More important things were waiting to be done, but with this project Pagnol had just begun to comment upon the entry of literature into the domain of cinema, and vice versa.[8]

From Jean Giono's novel *Solitude de la pitié* came Pagnol's 1934 *Jofroi*, a sharply defined cameo depicting the elderly hero's struggle to prevent his trees from being uprooted by their new owner. This would be the first of the collaborative efforts of Giono and Pagnol, which are examined in more detail under the aspect of adaptation in the following chapter. In commercial theaters *Jofroi* would often be shown with Pagnol's first work *Le Gendre*, forming an attractive diptych. Pagnol completed another short film *L'Article 330* in the same year and also provided Raymond Bernard with the scenario and dialogue for the adaptation of Alphonse Daudet's novel *Tartarin de Tarascon*.

Already one can detect the Pagnol Co. taking shape—the clever Hungarian Willy responsible for the photography; Vincent Scotto, the composition of the musical scores; Charles Brun, the artistic aspect of the film; and Suzanne Troye, the editing. Delmont, Raimu, Fernandel, Blavette, Poupon, and Demazis would each play out his or her role not only with theatrical sensitivity but also with a joviality that was characteristic of the Midi. Fernandel once described the family spirit behind their filming; he remarked that to make a film with Pagnol meant going to Marseilles, having a *bouillabaisse* with the gang, talking about the weather, and then, if there was some time left, doing a bit of filming.[9]

Giono's *Un de Baumugnes* offered a starting point for Pagnol's *Angèle* in 1934. Although filmmaking was still concentrated in the studio to provide optimum conditions, the cinéaste moved to the countryside as he did for *Jofroi*, and thus achieved a greater authenticity in his work. The film crew called their location "Angèle's farm," situated not far from Camoins in the Massif d'Alluch. Some of the shots were taken in Manosque as well as in Marseilles, where Saturnin (Fernandel) tries to persuade the wayward Angèle (Orane Demazis) to return home for reconciliation with the family.

Capitalizing on his knowledge, interest, and experience in the teaching profession, Pagnol turned once again to the classroom for inspiration, as he did with the play and film *Topaze*. In this next film, the terrifying teacher Merlusse (Henri Poupon) would be shown to have a heart of gold. During the Christmas vacation of 1934 and then again in the course of the summer vacation of 1935, Pagnol entered upon the familiar site of the Lycée Thiers in Marseilles to film his *Merlusse*. Pagnol, unhappy with the technical aspect of the original filming in 1934, requested a second shooting. *Merlusse* would certainly make a fine central panel in a triptych of classroom-oriented films with Vigo's *Zero de conduite* and Anderson's *If*.

Once upon a glorious time there was a chef who refused to condescend to cook for his clientele. Pagnol knew of this situation and made a film that described the predicament.[10] The first time he filmed *Cigalon* he used Henri Poupon as the principal character and Charles Blavette as the phony count who is served a four-star meal. Displeased with the results of the filming (another reshooting like *Merlusse*), the director went back and reworked the entire film with Arnaudy as the chef and Poupon as the client.

The remake would soon become a part of the philosophy of the director. Léopold Marchand made the first *Topaze* in 1932, Pagnol the second in 1936, and the third as well in 1950. These variations on a theme of tension between the teaching profession and the business world had as their base the 1928 play, but each added a new cast, for instance, Louis Jouvet, Arnaudy, and then Fernandel as the moralizing Topaze.

César (1936) marked Pagnol's personal touch to the Marseilles trilogy with *Fanny* of Allégret and *Marius* of Korda as the other episodes. Raimu would provide a brilliant interpretaion of César, the café-owner and father of Marius.

Most anecdotes surrounding Pagnol's filming emanate from the time of *Regain* (1937). For this film, Pagnol had Brouquier reconstruct an entire village on the model of Redortiers, which lies northwest of Manosque near Banon, and may recall the ghost towns of the southwestern United States. One neighbor asked the crew why they were building a village in ruins instead of a new one. On another occasion a curé passing nearby wished to say Mass in the chapel, the milieu appeared so realistic. For the sound track Pagnol did not wish to have the music "tacked on" to the film subsequent to the editing. Instead he asked Arthur Honegger to compose the score on location. For two months Honegger dedicated himself to this task, assisting with the incidental chores involved with the filming during the day, and then peacefully composing the music under the tranquil Provençal night sky. The outdoor concert must have been an unbelievable sight to behold—forty musicians performing the Honegger score for the film on the fragrant hillside, with art and nature in perfect harmony.

A few years prior to *Regain*, while the cinéaste was laboring over *Angèle* in the proximity of the recreated village of "Aubignane," a young man came up to the crew and began speaking with them. In a spirit of jest they told the young man he resembled Charles Boyer and should really be in film. They continued the prank, telling him that there was a role waiting for him in Paris, since Boyer was unable to accept it. The gullible fellow traveled to Paris to begin his film career.[11] This anecdote later served as the embryo of the film *Le Schpountz* (1938). Pagnol chose Fernandel to incarnate Irénée, the naive "Schpountz," a curious word that the cinéaste often found on the lips of the Eastern European photographer Willy. The victim would, however, score a success in the Paris film world, and his eventual return to his family in the provinces evoked the warmhearted welcome of a prodigal son.

That same year the director captured the overwhelming tragedy of an adulterous baker's wife as originally created by Giono. In *La Femme du boulanger* the minor incident in a little village takes on disastrous proportions, involving the entire populace. This ingenious adaptation would be the cause of strife between the cinéaste and original author, but would be one of the more popular of Pagnol's works.

On the eve of World War II, Pagnol filmed *Monsieur Bretonneau*. As he had done for his first feature film, Pagnol used a play, this time a light comedy of Robert de Flers and Gaston Arman de Caillavet as the departure point for this work. Despite the efforts of Raimu and Josette Day, this *ménage à trois* in boulevard style would leave something to be desired.

Besides *La Femme du boulanger* and the Marseilles trilogy, *La Fille du Puisatier* appears to be the most popular of Pagnol's works distributed internationally. The action takes place during the war when Patricia, the eldest daughter of the widower Amoretti, falls in love with an aviator on leave and soon finds herself with child. Love and war blend as delicate ingredients of a very controversial film. The film would have great success in the Unoccupied Zone of southern France, especially because of the sound track that preserved an original speech of Marshal Pétain, which caused Pagnol no little harassment later on.

During the war the Germans controlled a major part of the French film industry in Paris. At the same time films were being made in Nice, especially newsreels accentuating the patriotic themes of family and work in a Pétain kingdom. Refusing to comply with the occupying forces in 1941, Pagnol deliberately abandoned his work on *La Prière aux étoiles*. The film was never completed. In the meantime, Pagnol sold his stocks and studios for a paltry sum to avoid getting involved in the politics of cinema. He would not take up the camera again until after the war, although he did supervise Robert Vernay's *Arlette et l'amour* (1943).

The war terminated and Pagnol returned to his familiar film world and quickly became established. First he founded the Société Nouvelle des Films Marcel Pagnol. The producer/director asked Raymond Leboursier to film *Naïs* with Fernandel and a promising actress, Jacqueline Bouvier. The company, the film, and his relationship with the actress proved most successful and she became his wife on 6 October 1945.

Pagnol was involved in many projects as the postwar film industry grew. While still writing, he was directing and producing his own films, and supervising the studio and laboratory—truly a "Renaissance man" of the cinema. The château La Buzine that he purchased sight unseen for locations, happened to be the same château that he and his parents had earlier feared when they used to pass through this area on the way to their country cottage.[12]

La Belle Meunière (1948) and a remake of *Topaze* (1951) led Pagnol eventually to *Manon des sources* (1952), a subject that could almost originate in the pen of Giono. In this film, a family is almost exterminated because of the malicious conspiracy of some villagers to hide a spring. *Manon* glorifies the triumph of the just in the personage of the young heroine (Jacqueline Bouvier/Pagnol). The cinematic marathon of four hours, poetic as it may have been, had to be reduced by almost one hour for commercial distribution. The film was presented on French television in 1968 in eighteen episodes of thirteen minutes, the sign of renewed popularity.

For the finale to his filming career, Pagnol turned to one of his literary masters from the Midi, Alphonse Daudet, to film three tales of *Les Lettres de mon moulin* in 1954. "L'Elixir du Révérend Père Gaucher," "Les Trois Messes basses," and "Le Secret de Maître Cornille," serve as delicate moving photographs of the lyrical mélange of humor and seriousness of life in the south of France. The prologue with the character of Daudet entitled "La Diligence de Beaucaire" was eliminated in the shortened version, and other episodes envisaged by Pagnol were never filmed.

Aside from an occasional dabbling in television or cinema in the late 1950s and early 1960s, Marcel Pagnol hesitated to assume the responsibility to which he was accustomed in his long career. His reign of more than a quarter-century in the realm of the sound film would come to an end, proving to friend and foe alike of the 1930s, that sound was not a passing phenomenon. On 18 April 1974, Pagnol joined his eternal *copains*—Raimu, Fernandel, Delmont, and Poupon.

In the new edition (1977) of Georges Berni's brochure written in homage to Marcel Pagnol, a color centerfold depicts "Le Petit Monde de Marcel Pagnol," his familiar milieu created in *santons*, the famous wood-carved dolls of Provence.[13] In the background of the re-creation, fitting snugly among the stark, rolling hills, lie La Buzine, Pagnol's nineteenth-century château made famous in the memoirs *Le Château de ma mére*, and a composite Provençal village. Peopling this hamlet are the characters of Pagnol's literary and cinematic works, the gamut of citizens of the Third Republic (1870-1940). In the center foreground, naturally, some mustachioed villagers in shirt sleeves are engrossed in *pétanque*, with the local curé (Henri Vilbert) in full cassock and biretta, and an elegantly dressed teacher (Bassac) as spectators. To their left ensues a vigorous card game from the Marseilles trilogy with Raimu (César), Robert Vattier (M. Brun), and Charpin (Panisse). Fanny and Marius, with the characteristics of Pierre Fresnay and Orane Demazis, are directly behind the card players and in the shadow of Tante Honorine. Here and there other Pagnolian characters make their appearance—the knife- and scissors-grinder from *Regain*, the chef of *Cigalon*, the well digger, the rotund and ferocious-looking Merlusse, and the baker of *La Femme du boulanger*. Surveying this unique world is Marcel Pagnol himself in his customary red-checkered shirt, plume in hand, surrounded by his literary trinity—Vergil, Daudet, and Giono. This representation constructed in Aubagne, Pagnol's birthplace, testifies to what the director had gleaned from the provincial life of the Midi to which he was exposed for a significant part of his life.

A close examination of the elements that comprise Pagnol's cinema kingdom will indicate the cinéaste's power of observation, reconstruction, and dramatic suspense.

In 1963, Pagnol, while reminiscing, asked rhetorically what his films and plays speak about. In the same breath he gave his reply: "About bread, water, a mother, an illegitimate child, always very simple things-... with Dickens, Daudet, and Mistral as masters."[14] Pagnol could skillfully structure his filmed drama around the classroom, the village square, or a café at the Old Port of Marseilles. In the easygoing Provençal village or the seaport café, the eternal sun caresses the convivial characters who sip their licorice-tasting *pastis,* playing cards or *pétanque,* emitting with their garlic-flavored breath colorful allusions to the oldest profession in the world—their "putaings" dramatically interjected into their flowing pseudophilosophy or exaggerated anecdotes. As the cicada chant in the breezy mistral, the lavender and the rosemary fragrance enchants the village, while the smell of recently netted fish and the lamenting cries of the seagulls fill the seaside air. With their grandiose gestures and expressive imagery, one would think that these Provençaux were on stage, as indeed André Roussin, Pagnol's colleague at the Académie française, rightly observed, saying that Marseilles is a city where comedy plays as a permanent show.[15]

Who are these vaudevillian players who strut and fret their colorful hour upon the stage? Some are comic and tragic creatures who emerge directly from the Provençal life of Pagnol: The "Schpountz" who, arriving on the set for *Angèle*, believed he resembled Charles Boyer; the chef Cigalon who actually refused to cook for his customers; and Marius, a young poet acquaintance of Pagnol's who, wearying of the life in Marseilles, embarked for Australia.

Another group of characters are archetypes of certain attitudes, mannerisms, and values: The typical Provençal village curé of *Jofroi* who understands family dilemmas and serves as commentator or arbitrator; the administrator of a boarding school like the Machiavellian Oscar Muche; or a Pagnolian Topaze who abandons the sacred halls of the academic profession for more enterprising adventures. In the latter case, since both Pagnols, father and son, pursued this vocation of professor, the available descriptive models and anecdotes were legion.

The last series of characters like the primeval Panturle, Angèle, the suicidal Jofroi, or Saturnin, owe their inspiration to Giono. For Pagnol, nonetheless, each figure undergoes a metamorphosis in a reinvention of the original idea. The character ordinarily sketched in ethereal terms by Giono is made more concrete in the film—given the nature of the medium—fleshed out with particular physical features. Moreover, a more personal, human side of the individual comes to the surface as in *Regain* or *La Femme du boulanger*. Once the cinéaste flashes his comic or tragic heroes and heroines on the screen they become immortalized and function as types of certain tendencies in individuals. The phenomenon is circular: Pagnol draws his inspiration from the people around him, relying upon his astute sense of observation. He paints their portraits in a motion picture, as in the case of a César, the café-owner and father of Marius at the Old Port of Marseilles. Then the models become types, as the individuals represented take on a universal dimension. The portraits painted by Pagnol, although based on reality, are also touched up here and there with certain features highlighted. A perfect graphic parallel to Pagnol's treatment of his characters can be found in the popular posters of Albert Dubout, for example, as he depicts the burial of Panisse in *César* or the caricatured scenes of Fernandel in *Naïs* or *Schpountz*.[16] In the symbiotic relationship between filmmaker and the poster artist, the faces of actors of the caliber of Raimu and Fernandel become household furnishings. A comedian like Raimu would be the word made flesh, the spokesman of Pagnol, whereas Fernandel's smile preserved on celluloid would serve as an inspiration for future generations, says Pagnol.[17]

Pagnol's casting of characters in their natural cadre is alluring. At a time when "French cinema" meant in reality "Parisian cinema," the Provençal filmmaker ventured forth in his attempt to popularize the South of France in a more folkloric manner that would become an exoticism par excellence for the Americans as well as for the Parisians. Explaining his national and international success, the director remarked that the more the work was local, the more it could be taken for universal. With this maxim, states Gaston Bonheur,[18] Pagnol perhaps meant to say that the little dramas of life often take on grandiose proportions as in Balzac's *La Comédie humaine*. The literary Midi of Daudet, Mistral, and Giono reaches its physical zenith in Pagnol's concretization on film. Just as in the case of Giono, the cinéaste Pagnol, another weaver of tales, commences with an anecdote, vividly embroiders it, and then spins out an epic where tears and laughter oscillate as night follows the day.

Life in a slumbering Provençal village, the battlefield of a classroom, or the bustling seaport café is sown with tragicomic scenes that Pagnol gradually unfolds on screen. The direction he takes in sculpting these characters in context might be best referred to as "southern humanism," in the words of André Bazin.[19] When the artist graphically paints a Topaze, victim of the powers that be; a Manon and family almost annihilated by certain insidious villagers, especially Ugolin who, guilt-ridden, hangs himself in shame; a Schpountz, prey to malicious pranks of the film crew; or an expectant Fanny, whose love still lies with Marius despite his sudden departure, it is difficult not to sympathize with suffering humanity. On the other side of the coin, the verbal mock battles over paltry issues in *Marius* or the absence of logic in the obstinate Jofroi provide a moment of refreshing humor that is most characteristic of the Midi.

In his humanistic manner, Pagnol does not hesitate to moralize and satirize, accurately sketching the values and interests of the multileveled society. The question of suicide is taken up in *Jofroi, La Femme du boulanger*, and *Manon des sources*. Certain conflicts tragically bring the individuals to the threshold of death and sometimes beyond. With *Le Schpountz* we have another glimpse of society, this time the cinema world. Jean Laury in *Le Figaro* for 19 April 1938 considered this film a series of lectures on swindling practices in the cinema and on the responsibility of film directors, besides being a treatment of the traditional subject of love. The young teacher Topaze does not hesitate to offer lessons in morality to his students before his future employer seduces him into his unprincipled business affairs. A forgive-and-forget philosophy concludes *La Femme du boulanger* following upon the liaison of the unfaithful wife of the baker with the valet. In this sense, Pagnol's film career from *Angèle* to *Regain* parallels Rossellini's from the neorealistic to the didactic.[20] The problems that Pagnol touches upon are real and represent a significant cross-section of life in the south of France. For this reason, René Prédal in *La Société française à travers le cinéma* (1972) is justified in observing that Pagnol's films are just as "true to life" as those of the ethnologist-filmmaker Jean Rouche (*Les Maîtres-fous, Moi un noir, Chronique d'un été*). Recently in Cassis, a Provençal woman not quite fifty, with delicate olive skin and eyes to match her raven-black hair, illustrated the "ethnology" of Pagnol. Possessing a rich flair for imaginative expression, she lamented the passing of the good old days of Pagnol's Marseilles, a moment when it was still a "village." Familiar as she was with the "old" Marseilles and the area around Camoins where her grandparents used to live, she swore that Pagnol's films were neither caricature nor exaggeration. "C'est vraiment *nous*!" she confirmed, and then proceeded to illustrate her statement with two anecdotes—a casserole being passed on cords from one apartment to another across a narrow Marseilles street suddenly tumbles and offers the neighborhood mongrels "un-e grand-e bouf-fe" for the day; or a woman grocer, perturbed at another woman client who was pinching the fruit: "Hé qoui, Madam-e, est-ce que je touch-e les chos-es de votre mari?" A few more hours of southern leisure could reveal a litany of further examples of Marseilles life that reinforce the truth of Pagnol's cinema. Vittorio de Sica and Roberto Rossellini, the co-paternal founders of the neorealist movement are thus correct in attributing to Pagnol the original neorealist spirit that began with his 1934 film *Angèle*.[21]

With respect to film technique, Pagnol must be ranked among the pioneers at the dawn of the sound film in France. His experimentation with sound offered more confidence to directors of the silent film and created a greater demand for this novelty in cinema. Pagnol was very sensitive to sound in his film work, perhaps by reason of his interest in *hearing* the text in its absolute, perfect, communicable state. With funds from his earlier successes, Pagnol in 1934 was able to invest in his own studios and sound truck from Philips. As a result of this acquisition, during the shooting of a film he would be found more often in the sound truck than behind the camera, relying upon the actors' talents following the rehearsals and the technical skills and sense of improvisation of Willy and Roger Ledru, who were responsible for the actual filming. For *Angèle* Pagnol and Jean Lecocq attempted to create a fuller dimension in sound with "une perspective sonore." In the same film, remarks Claude Beylie, Pagnol utilized tinted film to effect a more realistic ambiance—blue for night scenes, pink for the daytime, and multicolored for certain particularly dramatic sequences.[22] Although Méliès would produce a color effect in his magical films a little more than a decade after the birth of the cinema at the turn of the century, and Jacques Tati would experiment with color tinting in *Jour de fête* (1947) Pagnol would be in the avant-garde of color films just as he was with sound. One of the first color films in France was Pagnol's *La Belle Meunière* (1948) made in a special process called "Rouxcolor."

With the rebirth of regionalism in France in literature, film, and language, Pagnol has suddenly been rediscovered. Yvan Audouard underlined this by indicating his contribution to *occitanisme.*[23] Pagnol's plays and films, despite the earlier controversies over the *théâtre filmé* and the popularizing of the local Marseilles image, not only reflect a brilliant picture of the Provençal populace but go beyond to capture the everyday tragedy and melodrama in the life of Everyman. His film opus, a poignant testament of values of a bygone culture, thus has become the vehicle of a certain mythology. From his Marseilles saga, through the satires of *Topaze* and *Le Schpountz* and his encounters with Giono, and then ending with his bucolic *Manon des sources*, Pagnol has made a statement about *la condition humaine* that amuses, instructs, but, above all inspires.

Korda/Pagnol: *Marius*, **1931.**

Gasnier/Pagnol: *Topaze*, **1933.**

Pagnol: *Jofroi*, **1934.**

Pagnol: *Regain*, **1937.**

Pagnol: *La Femme du boulanger*, **1938.**

Pagnol: *La Fille du puisatier*, **1940.**

4

JEAN GIONO

Writing is an art, whereas making films is an industry. To work with a pen is certainly more complicated than to work with a camera.

—*Preface to Crésus* (1960)

In his witty souvenirs of Marcel Pagnol, Yvan Audouard recounts a very illustrative anecdote about the playwright/cinéaste's confrère, Jean Giono. An American journal once asked Giono to describe the most extraordinary person that he had ever met. The novelist immediately set to work and came up with such a description. The Americans were delighted. When they arrived with their cameramen and wanted to make a film about this personality, Giono gently chided them, "Et vous voudriez en plus qu'il existe," or, "I wrote the description you asked for, and now you want such a character to really exist?"[1]

In essence, this situation indicates the major difference between Marcel Pagnol and Jean Giono. Pagnol, almost in an ethnological manner, *captures* in high relief the tragicomic Mediterranean world, an already existent, vibrant milieu, whereas Giono, in lyrical fashion, *creates* his own world. Although this divergence in their aesthetic vision is paramount, nonetheless there developed a very close affinity between the two literary filmmakers, each reflecting the glory of the other in his work. Considering Giono's relationship with the film in the form of thirteen screen adaptations from his own works, many others for television, several film scripts, his own direction of the film *Crésus*, and his presidency at the Cannes Film Festival, perhaps the most popular contact he had with the film was via Pagnol. They shared certain characteristics right from their birth, for they both came into the world at the dawn of cinema in 1895, under the same Provençal sun. Their destinies would cross especially as Pagnol adapted four of Giono's literary pieces for the cinema. The careers of Giono and Pagnol would thus overlap in the world of literature and cinema. Each would become a master of tale-telling; Pagnol would fascinate his audiences with his Marseilles epics, whereas Giono charmed with his cosmic overtones. As a result, the critics of the two would say that Pagnol could sense the heartbeat of humanity whereas Giono could reveal the heartbeat of the universe.[2] Their election to the literary academies (Pagnol to the Académie française in 1947 and Giono to the Académie Goncourt in 1954) would crown their successful literary careers.

The conjunction of the two artistic planets of Pagnol and Giono took place in 1933. Their fraternal relationship would continue until the death of Giono in 1970, as Pagnol remarked in a series of interviews he gave on television in 1973,[3] tarnished only slightly by the legal problems in 1941 over the film *La Femme du boulanger* and Giono's negative reaction to the filmmaker's "indelicate" handling of *Jofroi* in 1933. By analyzing Pagnol's adaptations of Giono's novels and short stories, as well as the other directors' attempts to convey the poignancy of the written text on the screen, we can reach the heart of the creative and adaptive process of Giono, illustrating how his narrative took its roots in his Provençal reality, was transformed into a literary piece, and then made its way to the film and on occasion to the stage.

In the latter part of 1932, Pagnol was able to procure the rights for several films that would be adapted from Giono's opus, in particular *Regain, Un de Baumugnes, Jean le bleu, Colline,* and *Le Serpent d'étoiles.* Within the next few years the first three works as well as *La Femme du boulanger* would find a film public, and episodes of Mediterranean life would be amazingly re-created by the native sons of the Midi—Fernandel, Blavette, Raimu, Delmont, and Poupon, who would become archetypes of certain behavior.

Jofroi (1933-1934)

Long before ecology came into vogue, Giono and Pagnol collaborated on a film dealing with this topic that would mark their first joint venture. The actual incident preceding their literary and cinematic works took place between Manosque and Volx. Giono's friend, M. Redortier, purchased a plot of land and intended to cut down several barren trees on the property. The previous owner protested, threatened suicide, but eventually died a natural death. From this anecdote emanated Giono's story

"Jofroi de la Maussan," first published in 1930 and later in the collection of stories in *Solitude de la pitié* (1932).[4] Through Giono's embellishment of the event M. Redortier becomes Fonse and the original proprietor, the elderly and stubborn Jofroi. In this story-within-a-story framework, Fonse approaches the narrator to unburden his woes. The locale is shifted to Riez, ten to fifteen miles east of Manosque. Physical threats and numerous suicidal attempts soon fill the atmosphere. In the same tone, Giono accentuates the tragedy of the impasse by highlighting the frustrations and rigidity of Jofroi and the guilt feelings of Fonse.

Pagnol undertook the adaptation of this ten-page short story in 1933 and made of it a film of approximately one hour.[5] The material was expanded and organized into sixteen major sequences, as the scenario indicates.[6] The situation in the film takes on the grave proportions of Giono's story, but there is an undercurrent of comedy included, especially in the characterization of the obstinate central figure Jofroi and of Barbe, his elderly wife. Pagnol's choice of nonprofessional, Provençal actors such as Vincent Scotto[7] and Henri Poupon offered a heightened sense of authenticity. The same harsh, weary faces of *Jofroi* could easily be seen in a film such as Bergman's *Wild Strawberries*. [8]

Very sensitive to how a filmmaker should adapt his literary brain child, Giono was far from pleased with Pagnol's rendition of *Jofroi*. He accused the director of treating the short story not amicably but savagely, devouring and transforming the literary piece. This first negative experience, however, would not prevent them from continuing their collaboration.

On 28 December 1941, the troupe Le Chariot performed Jean-Pierre Grenier's adaptation of *Jofroi* for the stage at the Théâtre Municipal in Aix-en-Provence. In the preface to this one-act play, Giono congratulated the troupe for restoring to the play, "its buoyancy as well as its depth,"[9] alluding to his disappointment with the Pagnol version. It is not certain whether Giono felt some anxiety toward Pagnol at the moment of the release of the film or after their temporary falling out subsequent to the "Femme du boulanger" episode. The latter could have easily colored the novelist's feelings toward the adaptation. At its showing in Manosque, nonetheless, Giono was amused by the film and brought together the original characters who inspired the tale.

Angèle (1934)

Within less than a year of the first adaptation of a work by Giono, Pagnol produced and directed the second, based on the novel *Un de Baumugnes*. Somewhere between the age of six and eleven, Giono accompanied his mother to Remoullon, south of Gap, for a short vacation. The novelist recounts his experience there: "A young girl left home with a fellow from Marseilles. She soon returned with a child. Her father then had her hidden away in the cellar, and the whole village became interested in the girl."[10] Needless to say, Giono's very protective mother withdrew him from this scandalous environment.

With this kernel of truth Giono fabricated his novel of 1928,[11] vacillating betwen the titles *Celui des terres hautes, Celui des hauts villages,* or *Un de Beaumugnes* [sic]. Amédée, the bearded bohemian worker, becomes solicitous of the young Albin when the latter falls in love with Angèle. Louis, the archetype of Evil, however, lures her from the family farm to the fleshpots of Marseilles, where she becomes a prostitute. Disillusioned and denied of "virtue," she returns to the farm with a child, but is kept guarded in the cellar until Amédée discovers this and alerts Albin. The young man arrives to lead her away secretly by night, but en route decides to return with her to the father's farm following the advice of Amédée, so that the couple could begin their new life properly with the parents' blessing.

Giono invented the name "Douloire" for the farm that lay about five miles north of Manosque. The touching story of the villagers with their tongues slit also had its source in his imagination, whereas the locale "Baumugnes" was chosen for its heavy sound, the name having been taken from a signpost. The character of the elderly, itinerant laborer was plucked by Giono from the countryside and refashioned in *Les Grands Chemins* and *Solitude de la pitié*. The tale was narrated, as in *Jofroi*, suggesting an ambiance rich with suspense, ritual, and human sentiment.

The year the novel was published, André Gide wished to have it adapted for the screen. Marc Allégret and Alberto Cavalcanti would try to get an offer for the adaption from one of the German film directors gathering at the time in Bonn. The attempt was unsuccessful, and it was then that Pagnol chose to direct the film, having thought of adapting the work in 1932, even before *Jofroi*.

In the screen version, Pagnol not only translated the material but transposed and interpreted it, discovering a new freshness in Giono's original story. To an already moving work Pagnol added more sentiment, played down Amédée's role, and accentuated that of the handyman Saturnin (Fernandel) who became Angèle's confidant.[12] Much of the metaphor and mystery was eliminated. The action and characterization became more humanized, and the *angélisme* was more concretized. The father, Clarius Barbaroux, took on a rational, patriarchal temperament, becoming less severe than in the novel. The relationship of Albin and Angèle developed spontaneously, although it still retained some vestiges of sentimentality found in Giono's work.

Regain (1937)

The apogee of the Giono/Pagnol collaboration is attained with this ambitious film on the rebirth of an abandoned village. In the novel[13] of 1930 and in the film, this deserted hamlet is called Aubignane (from *Aubign*osc and Simi*ane*), but in reality it is Redortiers, situated northwest of Manosque near Banon. These ghostlike villages of southern France fascinated Giono ever since he had first seen Redortiers in 1906 or 1907, and then again just prior to World War I. After the war he witnessed "les derniers moments" of the village as the inhabitants gradually took their leave of it. The people there had lived in a savage state, spoke little, and had strange customs—not unlike the atmoshpere of Buñuel's *Las Hurdas*.

Leaning toward a pantheist ideology, Giono poignantly depicted the optimistic cooperation of man and nature, and more decisively, of a man (the colossal Panturle) and a woman (Arsule) in the resurrection of the community. Man is the initiator in this life full of new hope and promise. Giono indicated, however, the possible side effects of this regeneration: "A human civilization once established upsets and engulfs the savage glory of the earth."[14] Situated somewhere between Millet's *Angelus* and Vergil's *Georgics*, the sweeping images of primordial life elevate the story to the cosmic level: fecundity (Arsule's pregnancy at the arrival of spring), sustenance of life (wheat/bread), and lyrical sensuality (man's basic need for woman).

In the film *Regain*— the title indicating the grain that grows again after the cutting—Pagnol sensitively handled the text. The director took the death/life parable of Giono and found its equivalent in cinematic poetry. He demanded the authenticity found in the literary text, rebuilding brick by brick the entire village of Redortiers, as noted in the chapter on Pagnol. The elaborate project was completed by a crew of fifteen masons and a large group of electricians, carpenters, and mechanics.[15] The neighboring villagers soon referred to their site as "Village des poètes," or "Village Pagnol."

Pagnol's film closely follows the basic movements of the novel and captures the seasonal changes with the renaissance of the earth as a climax. The cinéaste concludes with Panturle's reference to the soil as "a land of goodwill," and a shot of the rich earth flowing to both sides of the plow. This image of the coming of spring would rival the lyrical spirit of Dovzhenko's *Earth*.

In an adaptation such as *Regain*, language has a significant place. Here the characters speak a type of syncopated, rustic poetry that suggests the primordial tone of Giono's novel. It succeeds for the most part, save for the moments when the Parisian accent of Gabriel Gabrio (Panturle) is noticeable. Be that as it may, this defect is lost in Giono's overall primitive world as remolded by the filmmaker.

La Femme du boulanger (1938)

On the international scene, perhaps the most popular of the Pagnol/Giono films, *La Femme du boulanger*, caused nevertheless the most tension between the two artists. In a manner of speaking, it is a film that evolved the most drastically from its original source. In 1953, Giono recounted to Jean Amrouche and Marguerite Taos the inspiration for his literary work. In about 1905 or 1906, there occurred a scandal in Manosque centered around the grocer and transportation manager Pascal. His wife one day suddenly stole away with another man. From door to door Pascal bewailed his sorry plight. Eventually she returned to the village but refused to enter the house until the curious villagers went back into their own homes. They complied, and Pascal and Fanny thereafter resumed their family life.

From this actual occurrence Giono embroidered a charming tale and published it in 1932 in *Nouvelle Revue Française* (*N. R. F.*) under the title "La Femme du boulanger." In the same year Grasset published the author's autobiographical novel *Jean le bleu*, and this incident became the nucleus of Chapter VII, "Le Boulanger, le berger, Aurélie."[16] Giono's treatment of the original episode demonstrates an intensely personal sensuality that may also be seen in the primeval *Regain*, but here it is presented in an already socially structured community. The written anecdote describes Aurélie's enticement of the shepherd, her riding off with him (seen through the eyes of Taille-fer-Patience), César's concern for the source of bread in the village, and finally the instructor and curate's search for the baker's wife. With her reappearance, life resumes its normal, Mediterranean pace.

Not too long after Giono's publication of the short story in *N.R.F.*, Pagnol considered making a film about an habitual inebriate named Amable. Eventually the poor creature marries, and love cures him of this social disease. Pagnol, returning one day from Belgium by train, stumbled across Giono's story in the *N. R. F.* He reread these fifteen pages three times, discovering there "a rustic *Iliad*, an epic that is Homeric and Vergilian at the same time."[17] That day he renounced his drunken Amable to re-create the Giono masterpiece that he would film under the original title in 1938. The scenario for the approximately two-hour film would be completed in eight days.

The humor and tragedy that are characteristic of Pagnol's works achieve epic proportions here: one man's experience of being cuckolded affects the entire hamlet, which desperately pleads with the baker for its "daily bread." Giono's original scene is expanded and the problem enters a plane in which socioeconomic and psychological factors dovetail. Class ideologies of the Third Republic are in conflict, incarnated by the personalities of the young, inexperienced clergyman and the free-spirited lay instructor.[18] In terms of characterization, the accent shifts from the seductive Aurélie to the malcontent Amable, largely because Pagnol had written the female role (one hundred forty-four words) for the American actress Joan Crawford, who spoke little French. Eventually when Crawford was unable to accept the part, Ginette Leclerc filled the role.

The general tone of the film is reminiscent of the fabliaux of old wherein the dedicated husband is duped by the voluptuous, unfaithful wife. The characters of Pagnol, too, have the same universal traits as a Misanthrope or an Arnolphe of Molière, and these characteristics come alive especially in the baker played by Raimu—the actor of many faces who knew how to play upon every emotion of the spectator.[19]

The next act in the "Boulanger" drama was the lawsuit of October 1941 described in considerable detail by C. E. J. Caldicott.[20] Giono felt that Pagnol had plagiarized his work in filming *La Femme du boulanger* and thereby broke their original contract of 1932, calling for their collaboration on the adaptations mentioned earlier—but not this film—and Giono's promise of a scenario in each case. The decision went against the novelist, since his not working with Pagnol on the adaptations freed the filmmaker of any responsibility in the contract. As a result, Giono was obliged to pay nine tenths of the legal expenses and Pagnol one tenth for having made use of the original title of Giono's short story.

Their collaboration, unfortunately, would end on this sour note, but their friendship continued. In the meantime, the exotic scenes of their shared projects created a sense of nostalgia for a paradise lost—the intimate Old Port of Pagnol quickly evolving into a cosmopolitan labyrinth and the universe of Giono developing a more obvious insensitivity to the rhythms of nature. With their cosmic reflections and creations, both literary filmmakers conversed with universal man. Giono, manifesting the spirit of an earlier Pagnol, philosophically observed that if someone lived in a certain region and spoke about this area while talking about himself, it was as if he were speaking about the whole world.[21] This literary and cinematic synecdoche would only be fully appreciated in the renaissance of a regionalism that these co-fraternal humanists would not witness in their lifetime.

Le Bout de la route (1948)

After Pagnol's final production of one of Giono's works, the stage was empty for ten years. No one attempted to adapt a selection from Giono's vast repertoire until Emile Couzinet planned an adaptation (from theater to screen) of *Le Bout de la route*. This would be the only film made from Giono's few theater pieces, for the 1941 stage version of *La Femme du boulanger* followed the film version.

In 1937, Giono published *Le Bout de la route* in *Les Cahiers du Contadour*.[22] It was first performed during the Occupation in 1941 at the Théâtre des Noctambules under the direction of Pierre Leuris with the collaboration of Vandéric and Pierre Gautherin. The young Alain Cuny was chosen for the principal role of Jean.

The material essentially borders on the melodramatic. In the setting of an eternal triangle, Jean (the itinerant do-gooder) arrives on the scene to interrupt the already existing relationship between Mina and Albert. Jean, who perceives that he would be interfering with the friendship of Mina and Albert, selflessly takes leave. This is not yet the end of the road for him, Giono concludes.

The play itself does not possess the richness and poetry of the novelist's prewar literature, although a bit of mystery momentarily appears through the veneer of Jean's character. The dialogue is often stilted and sentimental, but manages to keep the action moving.

Emile Couzinet, who, like Pagnol, knew the cinema from every angle, came originally from a tradition of filmed vaudeville and melodrama. He fared no better in the film adaptation than Giono on stage. Maintaining the spirit and overall movement of the theater version, Couzinet transposed the setting from the Haute Provence of Giono to the Hautes Pyrénées of Roland and Charlemagne. With mountains and lake as a backdrop, the director had greater liberty to exploit the visual image. His idyllic world—not dissimilar to a postcard setting—is populated by young men and women, for the most part handsome or beautiful, and very athletic-looking.

On screen the techniques, text, and decor have a hollow ring. The authentic experience of Jean's dilemma is overshadowed by the surrounding artificiality. The peal of the Angelus, the cock announcing the break of day, and the sun majestically showing itself in all its pristine glory over the mountains cannot be reproduced effectively on stage to indicate Nature's awakening; but here, on the other hand, the film director perhaps overstresses this *correspondance* (à la Baudelaire) of the various forms of nature. At the film's end, Berlioz's "Invocation à la Nature" blends with Jean's singing, while a series of superimposed shots of nature passes before the spectator. In this emotional atmosphere, Jean continues his venture. The exploitation of sentiment, very common in the films of the 1940s and 1950s, comes to a peak in the finale.

Utilizing techniques that would not be possible on stage, one may validly and richly translate dramatic material to the screen, as, for instance, Tennessee William's *Cat on a Hot Tin Roof* or *A Streetcar Named Desire*. In the case of this dramatic piece, the original material of Giono did not possess the usual high quality and poignancy, and the adapter took it further into the depths.

L'Eau vive (1958)

Giono, discussing in 1958 the previous adaptations of his work, remarked: "I have always been disappointed, for no matter how good the adaptation could possibly be, not one has corresponded to what I had envisaged. The only exception I would make is *L'Eau vive*."[23]

Through his affiliation with François Villiers, Giono initiated in 1955 a collaboration that would occasion three films—one feature-length (*L'Eau vive*) and two shorts (*Le Foulard de Smyrne* and *La Duchesse*). Prior to these projects, as in the case of Pagnol and Couzinet, the author witnessed the adaptation and filming process from afar, as if through a glass darkly. With *L'Eau vive*, Giono was lured into the production of the film, from the very germinal seeds of the work to its release and screening at the Cannes Festival.

The Giono-Villiers adaptation—also differing from the previous ones—would begin even before a written text existed. In 1955, Electricité de France was planning a dam on the Durance River at Serre-Ponçon. The estimated time necessary to construct the dam was five to ten years. In the meantime, the air was filled with negative publicity emanating from ecologists and traditionalists alike. Giono, with François Villiers and Alain Allioux (both from Films Caravelles), and Electricité de France arrived at an agreement to make a film that would depict the actual building of the dam and would simultaneously tone down the adverse reaction to the proposal.

Initially Giono and Villiers spent a considerable amount of time drawing up plans for the film, anticipating a period of five years for its completion. Together on location they first uncovered the various problems arising from the technological developments and drew up a list: irrigation, displacement of an entire village (Ubaye, southeast of Gap), invasion of technology in the countryside, and so on. Giono would narrate these problems in a realistic fashion at the outset of the film, and Oncle Simon (Charles Blavette) would be his spokesman—someone from the region who gradually came to understand the necessity of change.

François Villiers recounts their original intentions in this manner:

> *L'Eau vive* is not a full-length documentary, nor is it a romanticized story, pure fiction. *L'Eau vive* is a synthesis of human problems

> presented in a dramatized form, a synthesis which takes into consideration two principal characters whose destinies are always parallel and occasionally intertwined—a river (La Durance) and a young girl (Hortense).[24]

The two stories were in effect intermingled, for the family of the young Hortense attempted to snatch the heritage amassed by her father Félix when he sold land to prepare the way for the dam. The parallel of the two heroines would be marked by a "symbolisme discret," to cite Villiers's expression in this same article. In the end they would both be victorious: Hortense, like Antigone, would never submit to the manipulations of her family, and the Durance River would continue to flow freely once again.

Giono provided the scenario and the dialogues, whereas Alain Allioux took charge of the technical adaptation. Allioux's synthesis corresponded perfectly to Giono's expectations. The action would move on several planes: the epic (construction of the dam and inundation of Ubaye), the social (cultural problems in the displacement of individuals with certain traditions), and the psychological (the greed manifested by the family toward Hortense's inheritance).

In 1956, the filming began as the bulldozers confronted the mammoth task of preparing a site for the dam. Two key actors were chosen—Charles Blavette from Manosque, a familiar face in all of the Giono-Pagnol films, and Pascale Audret, a brilliant performer in the French production of *The Diary of Anne Frank*.

Above all, Giono and Villiers tried to create an authentic tone in the film. The names of the villages and cities that would be affected by the dam in one way or another were retained, such as Cavaillon, Ubaye, and Rochebrune. Blavette and the elderly actors spoke with an *accent méridional*. Many other members of the cast were filmed at work in their own fields or at the dam. A "cast of thousands" of sheep posed a problem of coordination with the actors, bulldozers, and weather. The five thousand bleating creatures, normally at home in pastoral surroundings, offered an added contrast to the dawn of the technological age, especially as they began to weave their way through the trucks and bulldozers, and later as they themselves flooded the streets of the village.

During the first year of shooting, approximately one third of the film was completed, concentrating on the early stages of the relationship of Hortense and Oncle Simon, the initial phase of construction, and the rerouting of the Durance. Filming ceased during the winter. Other actors and actresses, such as Germaine Kerjan and Andrée Debar, signed contracts and the shooting resumed in the spring of 1957. The major portion of the film was then shot. Up to this point the authenticity demanded by the filmmaker and the novelist had been achieved. Time and money, unfortunately, continued to flow all too quickly, and the snail's progress on the dam was discouraging. Meanwhile, the actors' contracts had to be respected; the insurance had to be maintained; and the movement of actors, technical crew, and equipment from one locale in the Haute Provence to another had already proved to be an expensive affair. After an investment of three years, Villiers decided to terminate the film, despite the fact that the dam remained unfinished and that Ubaye would not be inundated in the very near future. Models were, therefore, used to simulate the completed dam, and Hortense's place of captivity was rebuilt at the bottom of a swimming pool in Gap to create the illusion of the historical water burial of the condemned villages. The flooding would not take place until two years later. Claude Mauriac, who praised the film for its many favorable qualities, also shared the disappointment of the spectator at not having witnessed the actual climax of the colossal undertaking.[25]

The Giono-Villiers adaptation was apparently successful in the eyes of a few critics who referred to it as a poem, painting, or character study. Some delighted in the coupling of image and text to convey a philosophical message. Others, however, like François Truffaut, then a critic for *Cahiers du Cinéma*, felt that the film was impersonal and publicity-oriented in view of its financing by Electricité de France. In 1958, *L'Eau vive* was screened at the Cannes Film Festival with *Mon Oncle* (Jacques Tati), *O Saisons, O Châteaux* (Agnès Varda), and *La Seine a rencontré Paris* (Ivens/Prévert). Villiers, however, would not receive his just recompense until 1959 at the San Francisco Festival, where the film was successfully screened, entitled in English *The Girl and the River*. Hollywood would also offer him a prize the same year.

Following the completion of the film in 1958, Giono and Allioux published the dialogues.[26] They also decided to include the history of the ancestors of the characters, beginning with Martin Fabre in 1880, the period of Giono's parents. This publication marks the end of the lengthy and complicated evolution from the historical fact of the construction of the dam, through the planning phase, concretized in a scenario and adaption, and eventually filmed by Villiers. Observing Giono's participation in the project, even to the final stages of the editing process in order to verify the film's authenticity, one can easily understand why the results conformed to the author's expectations.

Le Foulard de Smyrne (1958)

In the meantime, creative inertia set in. While *L'Eau vive* was still in production in 1957, Giono and Villiers agreed to film a series of thirteen short stories, the scenario in each case to be provided by Giono. The two artists would be at their best in this cooperative effort, the succinct imaginative work being the specialty of both.

The first film in the series was *Le Foulard de Smyrne* dealing with an epidemic of cholera in Provence in 1832, a subject befitting Camus (*La Peste*). This period, during which Giono's grandfather Jean-Baptiste lived, fascinated the writer and offered him abundant material for short stories and novels. The subject of the cholera epidemic in the nineteenth century, for example, recurs intermittently in Giono's writings over a period of twenty-five years.[27] Professor Redfern regards the "Angelo" series of the novelist's work (*Le Hussard sur le toit*, "Angelo," *Mort d'un personnage*, and others) as different stages of character development of the Stendhalian hero who passes through cholera-infested areas, pursuing a life of heroism.[28]

The short film begins with Giono's narrative, "On 20 July 1832, at noon, a man steps down from his porch, takes a few steps and drops dead. He had cried out, "I'm cold!" and had run toward the sun, and yet it was an incredibly hot day."[29] An itinerant salesman unknowingly sells infected scarves, contraband from a boat originating in Asia Minor and then quarantined in Toulon. With the continued sale of wares, the epidemic spreads about the countryside until the vendor himself dies. The final scene shows the cemeteries that harbor the victims of the cholera.

Succinctness and stylization mark the presentation of the details of the narrative. The spectator sees only an umbrella sheltering the face of the vendor as he scurries about his business. Here and there on the screen appear a hand or a foot of a victim, the remains of a meal, or the infected scarves, but never a full view of any of the characters. When someone is struck by the germ, the image is frozen on the screen. For example, as an old woman drops dead in the initial sequence of the film, the subjective camera "looks up" at the crucifix and "falls." Later, as the epidemic intensifies, the entire screen gradually turns blue. With a clever legerdemain the scarves are made to disappear by their own power into the bag of the vendor, whom we see approaching from three different angles simultaneously to suggest his omnipresence. Throughout the film the suspense is perfectly maintained.

In August 1975, during our personal interview with François Villiers concerning his work with Giono, the filmmaker stressed the significance of *Le Foulard de Smyrne*. It is art in its purest refined state—that of *suggestion*, Villiers observed. In the film we note that the director does not depict concretely, but simply hints at the character traits of the vendor going about his lethal affairs. In its succinctness and resonance the work can be considered equivalent to a sonnet or a Japanese haiku.

Villiers further remarked in the interview that this short film illustrated what could eventually be done on screen with a longer, more complex literary text such as *Le Hussard sur le toit* which had been planned originally by the two artists.

La Duchesse (1959)

Since his youth, Giono entertained a vivid fascination with history, especially of the nineteenth century. The anecdotes passed along orally in his family, coupled with his own diligent research, made history very personal and alive for him. The second film in the Giono-Villiers series of shorts testifies to this.

The action of *La Duchesse* occurs at approximately the same time as that of *Le Foulard de Smyrne*, "une curieuse époque," according to Giono's commentary. In 1831-1832, the duchess of Berry—the Amazon of the Legitimist party—clandestinely entered France from her exile and attempted to organize an insurrection against Louis-Philippe. Her enterprise had little effect in Provence, and she was later imprisoned at Blaye. The film deals with an incident during her attempt to remove Louis-Philippe from power and with the door-to-door investigation that followed it. The spectator observes the latter proceedings from between the kepis of the two investigating officers.

As in *Le Foulard de Smyrne*, there is never a frontal view of the characters, and once again, suggestion prevails. Filmed on location in Provence, the work has an authentic touch. The historical sensitivity of the spectator is not abused by an attempt to reproduce *realistically* the costumes, locale, and mannerisms of the nineteenth century. The mysterious night scenes, the quick-paced editing, and the picturesque sites around Manosque and Verdon make the film a poetic piece of art.[30]

The year 1959 would signal in Giono's film career an abrupt end and a fresh beginning. *La Duchesse* would be the last film of the Giono-Villiers collaboration. At the same time, Giono and Andrée Debar (actress of *L'Eau vive*), with a hint of commercial enterprising, founded La Société des Films Jean Giono, which would be reponsibile for the production and distribution of films adapted from Giono's literary repertoire. Instead of resolving some of the technical problems, the enterprise created a few more, notably between Giono on one hand and Villiers and Clert of Caravelles on the other. The original agreement of the trio was to film *L'Eau vive, Le Hussard sur le toit,* and *Un Roi sans divertissement*. For financial reasons they were unable to produce *Hussard*, but the organization of the new corporation would now take any further filming of Giono's works out of the hands of Villiers as director and Films

Caravelles as producer. The specter of *La Femme du boulanger* reentered Giono's film career and a subsequent lawsuit terminated in damages paid to Villiers and Caravelles. On the level of personal relationship, as with that of Pagnol and Giono, the friendship of Giono and Villiers continued, and the filmmaker would thus pay homage to the novelist at his death in October 1970: "There is not a single shot from our three films that was not researched, discussed (often in great detail), and finally decided upon together."[31]

Crésus (1960)

With utmost modesty, Giono spoke of *Crésus* as a simple, unpretentious film that would certainly not revolutionize the cinema world or make a landmark in film history: "I simply had a story to tell, and this time I wanted to use a camera instead of my plume."[32] In this way Giono became a "filmmaker," although never abandoning his literary career, a point that the novelist would constantly reiterate to his interviewers at the time of filming *Crésus*. The experience that he gained working side by side with Villiers would now come to fruition.

The plot of the script, first written in 1957, is without complexity. The shepherd Jules Sauvat discovers a cache of counterfeit 5,000-franc bills in an unexploded, German bomb following the war. Not unlike Aurélie's disappearance in *La Femme du boulanger*, this incident transforms the tranquil ambiance of the hamlet. Meanwhile, the shepherd's relationship with the neighborly widow Fine begins to cool. Jules throws a banquet fit for the Croesus of old and then begins distributing his wealth. As can be expected, the people mistrust his generosity. Finally, two policemen inform him that the bills are counterfeit, and they recover all the money. All's well that ends well, for soon the hamlet is restored to normal, and Jules tells Fine that he will at last be her husband.

On the surface, the narrative sounds contrived and naive. Giono, nevertheless, has wedded here many fragments of a philosophy and morality, especially delving into the relation of financial abundance and happiness. In this peasant farce, the scriptwriter elaborates on the demystification of money. With a touch of bitter realism, Giono suggests that generosity will only bring with it unhappiness.

Insofar as the technical aspect of the film is concerned, the leap from a script to the actual shooting is a major one. Hence, Claude Pinoteau provided the novelist with the technical assistance necessary for the direction of the film as he also did with Cocteau for *Le Testament d'Orphée*. As usual the Midi—Forqualquier, Le Contadour, and so on—serves as a picturesque backdrop for the tale. The magnificent panorama is exploited to its fullest; the famous open-air banquet on the hilltop, with large, cumulus clouds in the background, could vie with Bergman, Dreyer, or Eisenstein scenes. Many of the interiors were shot in a studio for controlled conditions, and occasionally in an actual house. A realistic flavor is added to the drama by the naturalness of the Mediterranean accent among the characters who are mostly elderly, and by the original sites bordering Manosque. It is the behavior of the people and their bizarre predicament, however, that elevate the tone of the film from the real to the "sur-real."

The comic potential of the cinematic work of *Crésus* is resourcefully exploited. Fernandel, after thirty years of acting and incarnating a full gamut of characters, assumed the responsibility for the role that added humorous charm to the film. The discovery of the bomb, Jules' visit to the microscopic bank, Fine's destruction of the kitchen, the story of the "zeroes" in the classroom, the feast, and the mysterious hole dug as a cache for the bills are all scenes that provide a comedy of situation in its purest form. To balance this humor, the action is situated in a semi-tragic cadre, amidst the psychological tension and ennui of the village.

Despite Giono's fascination and work in a relatively young medium, he still managed to maintain his distance, oscillating between curiosity and misapprehension. His preface to the published script offers an insight into his attitude.[33] In this preface Giono considers writing an art, and cinema an industry, to use Malraux's terminology in his celebrated essay on the psychology of cinema. Noting the facility of making a film as opposed to the solitary challenge of writing (shades of Mallarmé), Giono decries the attitude of the "jeunes Turcs" who take the easy way out in film direction as well as those who are more materialistic and glory-minded. Giono resembles Pagnol here, another *homme de lettres* who viewed cinema as subordinate to the profession of writing, as we already observed in Pagnol's acceptance speech at the Académie française. Giono at one moment commented to Pierre Audinet:

> Only on occasion am I a cinéaste. Writing for me is a pleasure which I experience every day, whereas I consider filmmaking mainly a chore. It is a type of work which I feel I am too old now to pursue. On the whole, to adapt one's own book for the screen requires so many personal sacrifices that I prefer to relegate this task to others.[34]

Les Grands Chemins (1962)

A familiar sight for Giono was the farmhand in the Midi of France who moved with the seasons and the harvests, created lasting friendships with his fellow laborers, and worked until he was bored or had earned sufficient funds. *Un de Baumugnes* colorfully sketched the rapport of a pair of such workers, Amédée and Albin. Giono touched up the portrait of this duo twenty years later, achieving a delicate psychological study of the pair. It is a tale of a wise man and an impetuous, artistic youth.

Giono's novel *Les Grands Chemins* begins with the middle-aged mechanic-narrator relating his meanderings from village to village in search of work. One day he encounters a young man with a strange look in his eyes, who plays the guitar and cheats at cards. A frustrating association develops between them resulting from the instability of the young artist. Caught cheating at cards one evening, he is brutally beaten by the other players. Gradually he is nursed back to health through the efforts of the older companion, but when the youth mysteriously strangles an elderly woman, his friend feels it is his responsibility to take the situation in hand, and he leads the hunt for the murderer. In the early morning he finally discovers the young man and, out of a sense of total sympathy and friendship, shoots him. "C'est beau l'amitié!"[35]

Just as film direction enticed Giono, although momentarily, from his literary métier, it did the same for an actor named Christian Marquand. In 1956, Marquand played a major role with Brigitte Bardot in what has been labeled the first "Nouvelle Vague" film, *Et Dieu créa la femme* of Roger Vadim. Six years later, Marquand and Vadim collaborated on *Les Grands Chemins*, this time with Marquand directing and Vadim serving as the technical advisor.

In the metamorphosis into another medium, Giono's poetic aura of mystery and friendship vanished. The filmmaker made a vain attempt to preserve the key tension of the relationship and also to develop simultaneously from the material a type of sophisticated Western, situated in the Haute Provence. François, who appears to be a little younger than the narrator of the novel and certainly less of a sage, leaves Nice to deliver a jeep to Grenoble. He meets the impulsive Samuel en route. Here Marquand introduced a new character, the twenty-four-year-old widow, Anna, who lost her husband in the Algerian War. When Samuel is mercilessly thrashed, she shelters the young man and subsequently is seduced by him. Another alteration of the orginal text occurs when Samuel strangles an old woman for laughing at his lack of dexterity playing cards, and then seeks vengeance by slaying the men who were responsible for his mutilation. This accent on sex and violence, according to several critics, resulted from Giono's affiliation with Vadim. The overall popularization of the ingredients of the novel, in any case, produced a film of mediocre quality.

Un Roi Sans Divertissement (1963)

Inspired by a quote from Pascal—"A king without the ability to get beyond himself is a miserable man indeed" (Pensée 142, Léon Brunschvicg)—and from fragments of nineteenth-century history in the Alps, Giono created a highly nuanced fresco with a remarkable richness and depth. At the time of the original composition (1946), a particular court case left its imprint upon the writer's psyche. Between 1942 and 1944, Doctor Petiot committed twenty-seven murders. Some of the details of the trial were transposed into Giono's novels. In the year of the trial, Giono completed a chapter of a work entitled "M.V.... Histoire d'Hiver," publishing it in 1947 in *Cahiers de la Pléiade* and in 1948 in its present form with Gallimard.[36]

The story within a story is situated in the snow-packed Alpine village of Chicilianne around 1843. Marie Chazottes has mysteriously disappeared and Captain Langlois has initiated an investigation. Several other villagers fall victim to the evil force. Frédéric discovers the body of Dorothée, one of the victims, and then comes upon the murderer. Once alerted Langlois finds the other bodies, tracks down the criminal, and slays him in cold blood. He then simply wishes to resign from his post. There follows the stirring wolf hunt where the captain kills the hunted prey with the same tenacity as he did the murderer. Years later, Langlois is settled down; he leaves the room one evening after supper and commits suicide.

In 1961, Jean Giono and Andrée Debar of the Giono Film Co. were in search of an "intellectual" director who would film this novel. They discovered François Leterrier who, like Marquand, made his mark as an actor. Robert Bresson had invited Leterrier to play the principal role in *Un Condamné à mort s'est échappé* (1956). Four years later Leterrier directed his first film, *Les Mauvais Coups,* based on Roger Vailland's novel. Leterrier's sensitivity, aesthetic sense, and pantheistic orientation, according to Andrée Debar, suited the needs of the producers. Giono adapted his own novel for the screen and offered suggestions as the filming began. By 28 September 1962, Giono's scenario was complete.[37]

The tone of the work changed along with Giono's revisions, and the director respected the modifications.[38] In the transfer to the screen the subject matter was trimmed and the action consolidated. The wolf hunt precedes Langlois's murderous act, which is not too dissimilar to the *acte gratuit* of Gide. The procurator plays a greater role in the adaption, and Langlois in the film version is younger than he is in the novel. The café owner Saucisse becomes Clara and enjoys a more significant relationship with Langlois. All of this is situated in an ambiance of suspense, for we are never allowed to enter into the mind of Langlois or to see the face of the mysterious assassin who slays his victims out of boredom.

The atmosphere, like the dialogue, becomes dense in the film. A more poignant mood is created by the correlation of the gray and rigorous weather with the sadness and the boredom of the villagers. Solitude, uniformity, and death prevail. The new version accentuates the psychological aspect of ennui, murder, and the transfer of guilt from the assassin to Langlois. The village itself where the film was made—Aubrac in Auvergne—manifests an authenticity beyond question, for the most recent house built in the area bears the date 1830.

The scenario and film reflect a concern of the collaborators for the impact of the visual image and color. The candlelight interiors are reminiscent of a Rembrandt, whereas Leterrier's splendid and subtle use of black, gray, and red—specifically called for by the scenario—remains unique. In the pale images of the opening sequence with the contrast of the black nude trees and the white virgin snow, the spectator is made to believe that the film is in black and white. The lush red of the valet's jacket shortly afterwards proves otherwise. The blood fetish throughout the film continues the preoccupation with the aesthetic use of this color.[39]

The film in a mystical and ritual manner touches upon the realm of the sacred. The French critic Jean Collet suggests that Giono's universe is one of pagan mysticism where the novelist himself is the high priest of a lost religion.[40]

Le Chant du monde (1965)

With this film by Marcel Camus, director of the prize-winning *Orfeu Negro* at Cannes in 1959, we return to the primordial milieu of untamed nature, so familiar in the early works of Giono. The original version, according to Giono, was written around 1931 and depicted a community of poor peasants directed by a priest. They experience a personal freedom simultaneously with a newly felt spiritual liberty. Unfortunately this manuscript, referred to by Christian Michelfelder in 1939, mysteriously disappeared from Giono's study.

In 1934, the novelist published the present text of *Le Chant du monde*.[41] Following the natural rhythm of the seasons, he traces the adventurous search of Antonio (Bouche d'or) and Matelot for the latter's son Dennis (Le Besson). En route they discover a blind woman, Clara, entrust her to "la Mère de la route," and continue on until they locate the son in the savage country lorded over by Maudru. Matelot is killed, and Clara joins Antonio. The son, his fiancée Gina (Maudru's daughter), Clara, and Antonio then plan their escape. Le Besson and Bouche d'or in a spirit of vengeance first burn the ranch of Maudru. They evade their pursuers by launching a raft upon the river. The two couples, filled with hope, plan to build a new life at the other end of the river.

In the primitive scene of the forest along the river[42] and the medieval setting of Rebeillard, Giono situates the myth and ritual with strong resonances—the powerful current of evil (Maudru and followers), the folk rites of life and death, and the mythology surrounding the river. Bouche d'or and Toussaint share characteristics common to the shaman in their sensitivity to the elements of nature and their liaison capacity between nature and the "layman." In general, harmony exists in the universe, but concomitantly the dissonance caused by the evil forces operative in life also causes endless tension.

The novel is complex and filled with unseen currents like the enigmatic river, patterned on the Durance. The names and places are often Provençal. The personage of "Mère de la route" is inspired by Giono's grandmother, whereas Toussaint the healer in reality is a M. Combes, an acquaintance of the young Giono. The character of a blind person such as Clara is common in Giono, as observed in the guitarist in *Naissance de la pitié,* and the vendor in *Que ma joie demeure*, and others, a preoccupation perhaps explained by the fact that Giono's mother lost her sight, and also by Giono's respect for the sensitivity of the blind, especially to touch.

In 1941, Giono had planned a scenario with the producer Garganoff, but nothing ever materialized and the film would have to await the eventual direction of Marcel Camus. This filmmaker recounts his interest in adapting the novel of Giono for the screen:

> From a very tender age as an adolescent, I have had a great fondness for all of Giono's work. I especially admired his novels where the powerful wind blows through the upper and lower Alps. I chose Giono for his love of life, his love of living, which should not be confused with passion.[43]

Giono was not involved in this adaptation, although Camus, out of courtesy, sent him a copy of the scenario. The director would be principally responsible for the transfer to the screen, without the guidance of the author, which had been so important to Villiers and Leterrier. In order to grasp the creative process at work in this adaptation, it would be advantageous to see what Camus kept of the original novel, what he transformed, and what he eliminated. At work here would not only be the aesthetic background of the adapter, but his talent, personal interests, and his intuitions in exploiting the visual medium to its fullest. In a sense, however, this may reflect more on the work of Camus than on that of Giono, but it still shows the vast visual potential of the novelist's literary piece.

Like the novel, the film is essentially one of action, but differs with the inclusion of elements of the Western, unfortunately intended by the cinéaste. Camus sings the pantheist hymn to nature in the style of Rousseau as the seasons continue to follow their course. It is man against the elements also—the obstruction by snow and the destruction by fire. With full, rich colors the film artist paints this struggle, erring only when he chooses to design blown-up postcards, as did Couzinet in *Le Bout de la route.*

The essence of the novel is there—the wild country, the major characters and their basic conflicts, the chase scene (which *begins* the film version), and the folk rituals. The blind Clara who is pregnant at the opening of the novel is simply sick in the film. Maudru's confidence man, *Maître d'école,* takes on a more striking personality in the film, developing fully this curious type of individual. Here and there the quasi-literary language with rustic overtones rings falsely, spoken by actors who come from everywhere but the Midi. The rite of spring turns into a carnival à la *Orfeu Negro.*

That which is lost, however, is most noteworthy. First, the omnipresent mystery that animates Giono's novel disappears. The meditative silence so important to the forest atmosphere is also put aside. Giono's lyric sensuality turns into a skin-deep sentimentality, especially in the tender and romantic scenes among the two couples. Redfern, in treating briefly the rich polarity of Giono's novel, speaks of the within and the without, tenderness and violence, meditation and action.[44] In the shift to the screen, Camus accentuates only one pole—the external aspect, the violence, and the action—and hence the film suffers from the absence of the dynamic tension inherent in the novel. Although something of the purity of the novel was lost in the adaptation, the film attracted many film enthusiasts and received the "Ticket d'or," awarded by the exhibitors for the best French film of the year.

The stage version of Giono's work, first planned by Jean-Pierre Grenier in 1958, was completed in 1968 under the title of *Le Cheval fou* and was performed in June 1971 by the students of the Paris Conservatoire. With the physical limitations of a stage, the work would have to undergo even a more radical change.

04 (1967)

With this short work Giono returned to the film industry after a certain period of disenchantment. At the end of 1965, when *Le Chant du monde* was still being screened in the movie houses of France, the Chamber of Commerce in Digne initiated plans for a film that would soon involve Giono. In order to replace the outdated tourist-oriented films made following the Liberation, in 1945, the Chamber of Commerce planned a more attractive and up-to-date film on the department of the lower Alps. Understanding the power and the extensive distribution that was possible in the media, the group intended to utilize such a film in France in order to enlighten visitors to the natural wealth and beauty of this *département*, designated 04. The French and foreign tourists would be informed of the vast areas of the lower Alps that were suitable for camping, relaxing, convalescing, or establishing secondary residences.[45]

Within the scope of the twenty-minute film, the committee responsible for the work hoped to offer a general glimpse of the key places of interest in the *département* (Manosque,[46] Sisteron, Digne, the Pont Mirabeau, the Durance River, and so on). It would concentrate on the uniqueness of each site and follow the natural flow of the seasons, as Rouquier did in *Farrébique*. To avoid any chauvinism in the making of the film, the committee allowed Giono to choose each locale and to head the commission on the film's creation. He would also be responsible for selecting the musical accompaniment, furnishing the dialogues, and narrating the commentary. M. Serrin of Cinéson in Cannes would take charge of the technical side of the filming.

In the last stages of Serrin's shooting, Giono had the material screened, *after* which he wrote the scenario. This would be the reverse of his experience with the short film *Le Foulard de Smyrne*, which was drawn from a previously constructed scenario. In the notes on the film, Giono intended that the image should speak for itself, reinforced by the text only to avoid any ellipsis in the continuity.

The vast series of shots taken by Serrin was ample enough for a two-hour film. The picturesque scenes captured the mood of the various corners of the *département*. Occasionally the crew faced some difficulty with the weather during the shooting. At one point the autumn scenes posed a problem, and Giono suggested writing to François Villiers or Films Caravelles for the "rushes" from *L'Eau vive*. Although both films were made in thirty-five mm, Villiers's film was in Cinemascope, which prevented the use of the necessary shots in the short film. The crew improvised and had to be content with what they already had, unable to await another autumn.

This project resembles that of *L'Eau vive* in terms of its financing and its objective—the dissemination of a certain attitude directed toward influencing the spectator to look anew at the situation at hand. In such cases there is a fine line between art and propaganda, as can also be noted in Malraux's filming of *Espoir* during the Spanish Civil War. The president of the Chamber of Commerce of Digne underlined the power of the image in referring to the film *04* as a rich and valuable tool in developing tourism.[47] In great works of art such as Picasso's *Guernica*, Flaherty's *Louisiana Story*, or Hochhuth's *Deputy*, the propaganda element slips into the background. With a minor work such as *04* it is difficult to judge which aspect predominates. It is also not easy to assess the impact of the film without statistics from the local tourist bureaus and from numerous interviews with visitors to the region who had seen the film and had come to compare the image to the reality.

With this short film, interestingly enough on the *département* that was so dear to Giono, the novelist concluded his formal affiliation with film. He would continue to appreciate the film as a spectator as he had always done since the days of "Charlot," and to see films occasionally, as his daughter Aline mentioned in a telephone conversation with us concerning Giono's interest in the film. The break with the cinema would be a gentle one.

Thirteen adaptations for the screen and several for television,[48] all emanating from one author's pen, represent a substantial investment in the film industry. Left behind at Giono's death were creative seeds of film projects that never reached fruition. These show even further potential; for example, Pagnol's intention of filming *Colline* and *Le Serpent d'étoiles*, as well as Villiers's proposed collaboration for *L'Ecossais, Angelo*, and *Le Hussard sur le toit* (Buñuel later was considered a possible director of *Hussard*) came to naught, just as did the idea of adapting Juan Ramon Jiminez' *Platero y Yo* and Giono's *Les Ames fortes* and *Naissance d'une odyssée.*

From the novel to the scenario and then to the film with all its responsibilities and demands, Giono's film odyssey is long. Like his forebear Ulysses, there awaited him many deviations full of curious surprises and moments of disenchantment. In the end, only history will tell if his voyage was a success.

5

ANDRÉ MALRAUX

Given these [present technological] conditions, what should be our concept of art for the masses? Above all its equality must be preserved. What better way to achieve this qualitative development of art than to give it the maximum of conscience/consciousness.

—Regards *(July 1936)*

The *esprit créateur* that crowned the exotic life and fertile work of André Malraux was still evident in the septuagenarian until his very last breath, when suddenly his destiny became eternally intertwined with that of his revolutionary heroes Katow, Kyo, and Tchen. Malraux's death on 23 November 1976 elicited a string of titles that provides a flashback into the political, cinematic, and literary history of the past half century.[1] Novelist, art historian, aviator, Resistance hero, revolutionary, propagandist, cinéaste, philosopher, and minister of culture of France, Malraux found himself by chance and by choice at the crossroads of history, sometimes as witness, sometimes as participant. Like Cocteau, Malraux had skirted many isms—surrealism, expressionism, futurism, and communism—but he was never shackled to any one of them. Myths abound in the circles through which Malraux passed, and only time and history will dispel them. Jean Arc'houan has already busied himself with the process of demythologizing Malraux, balancing his canonizing qualities with perspective, which shows the esoteric Malraux as a simple thief of Khmer statuary and a grandiose purloiner of classical texts.[2] In Arc'houan's judgment, probably the worst aspect of this "Johnny-come-lately of the Resistance movement" is Malraux's mythomaniac penchant as he sculpts his heroes in his own image and likeness. In attempting an objective, historical perspective, however, it is important not to cast off the wheat with the chaff.

Among the many currents that flowed through Malraux's life, two can be distinguished for our purposes, the Spanish Civil War (1936-39) and the "Seventh Art," cinema, both intersecting in his only film *Sierra de Teruel* or *Espoir*, as it has come to be known. In *L'Intemporel,*[3] one of the last works that he published before transmitting to posterity his posthumous messsage in *L'Homme précaire et la littérature,* Malraux retained his interest in both this epoch and the medium, correlating art and cinema, while citing *Guernica* of Picasso and *Potemkin* of Eisenstein. The art odysseys of Malraux to Venice, Florence, Fontainebleau, and so on were televised from April 1977 on, five months after his death. His specter seemed to return from beyond the Styx to haunt us about the eternal and the ethereal beauty of art, this *antidestin* to which he consecrated the last quarter of a century, as he nervously chain-smoked his cigarettes and ideas end to end, one with another. In his usual witty and shocking manner, he quoted *L'Irréel* (p. 230) in attributing to the Venetians the original "invention" of cinema four centuries earlier, with their sense of color, decor, staging, and movement. His acute perception of the interrelationship of art and cinema was obvious. Finally, Clara Malraux's recent testimony *La Fin et le commencement* as well as Suzanne Chantal's *Le Coeur battant* records in a personal manner the import of the war and the cinema for Malraux in the festive but still polemic years during and following the Popular Front.

Malraux's passing in November 1976 engendered a period of national (and international) mourning marked by a cascade of events—commemorative addresses, the renaming of streets and pavilions, the printing of unpublished articles and reminiscences, as well as radio and television specials—before the final homage was rendered this legendary figure in the Louvre's Cour Carrée. One of the highlights of the week was a projection of Malraux's film *Espoir* as part of Antenne 2's *Ciné-Club.* Renaud Matignon refreshes our memory of this milestone in cinema history with his description of the work as an epic and grandiose fresco with striking "plastic beauty" that recalls Eisenstein.[4] Claude Mauriac, who has seen *Espoir* at all the major stages of its curious history—1939, 1948, 1969, and 1970—calls this semidocumentary one of the ten best or perhaps even "one of the five most beautiful films" in the history of cinema. Once again, just as in the case of Malraux's image and influence, it would be advantageous to try to discern the true status of Malraux the cinéaste and his aesthetic film work in the history of cinema.

Before Malraux embarked upon his only film venture during the Spanish Civil War, he had been interested in this medium for more than a decade, when cinema was still experiencing growing pains and was just learning to speak. To uncover Malraux's earliest contacts with the cinema is like stumbling into an archeological excavation where one must sift through one layer after another. Not all the materials are intact, hence there is still some mystery surrounding the first phase of Malraux's interest in film. In his correspondence with the author dating from May 1971, a fourfold pattern could be detected in his viewing habits before his debut with *Espoir*: the German expressionist film, the American comedies, the Swedish silent classics, and the Soviet revolutionary works.

André Malraux's earliest cinematic experiences can be linked with the avant-garde journal *Action* in the 1920s. Collaborators such as Jean Cocteau (well established in the "modern" theater), Louis Aragon (with André Breton keystone of the surrealist movement), Blaise Cendrars (poet and defender of cinema), Max Jacob (poet and painter), Antonin Artaud (mad, controversial, experimental playwright), and Tristan Tzara (founder of the Dada movement), all manifested some interest in radical, intellectual, and artistic expression, tinged with left-wing politics. The Swiss Cendrars, according to Malraux, would be the pivotal point for the group in its contacts with cinema. Their discussions on film may have been especially invigorating, given the group's intensity of expression. A cursory glance through *Commoedia* for the 1920s and 1930s would reveal the film menu for the Parisians at the time. With Ivan Goll's cultural soirées the seed was already well planted and nurtured in Malraux. During this fertile, revolutionary period Malraux visited Germany. In his 1922 and 1923 trips he came into contact with a radical current of German expressionist films. Parallel in mood to Malraux's farfelu period, which could almost be an extension of the Méliès works, the expressionist movement fostered eerie set designs and special light effects immersed in the exotic, grotesque, and macabre. The *angst* of postwar Germany found an outlet in the haunting works of Lang, Leni, Wiene, and Murnau—Malraux's patron saints of German expressionism. *The Cabinet of Dr. Caligari* by the Czech-born Robert Wiene impressed Malraux[5] just as it did Cocteau, and it would soon become a hallmark of a new aesthetic movement in film.

Before and well after the advent of the sound film in the late 1920s, the American comedians (or comics) experienced international celebrity. Humor like love was a universal language, and Malraux appreciated it, praising the works of Charlie Chaplin, Harry Langdon, and Buster Keaton. Most filmmakers in France (and perhaps in Europe in general) were nurtured on the Chaplin classics. A myth was soon perpetuated about "Charlot," especially among the French, who saw in this tragicomic figure of the tramp, the triumph of the will to survive despite society's obstinate efforts to snuff out the lowly creature. Malraux eulogized the comedian in *Esquisse d'une psychologie du cinéma*[6] describing a Chaplin film assembled from excerpts of his works, not unlike Richard Patterson's *Gentleman Tramp* (1976). Other American films seen by Malraux prior to filming *Espoir* were the gangster classics of the 1930s, such as *Scarface*. Carral's destruction of the Fascist cannon with the car in *Espoir* was an episode befitting a film in the tradition of *Scarface* or *Public Enemy*.

Ingmar Bergman's provocative films since the 1950s have dominated the Swedish film scene and have almost obliterated the reputation of his masters to whom Malraux had always shown deference. Two Scandinavian films of the early 1920s were especially appealing to the young Malraux: the Swedish director Victor Sjöström's *The Phantom Carriage* (1920) and the Dane Carl Dreyer's *Passion of Joan of Arc* (1928), starring Falconetti and Antonin Artaud. The long flowing movements as well as the atmosphere of the converging sacred and the eerie in these films were later to be found in Malraux's *Espoir*.

Very few films stand out as strongly in Malraux's aesthetic theories and works as Eisenstein's *Potemkin* (1925), which Malraux first saw in Berlin in 1927. This history-making epic of the 1905 Revolution in Russia was a work of such great stature that from the time of its showing the film was considered an art work. During the filming of *Espoir*, Malraux frequently spoke of Eisenstein and the social cinema, according to his assistant Max Aub in a private conversation with the author concerning the conditions of filming. For Malraux, Eisenstein was the paragon of film direction, a genius in whom art and politics perfectly coalesced. Besides *Potemkin*, Malraux by 1938 had already seen the filmmaker's *Strike, October,* and *The General Line*, along with other Soviet classics of Pudovkin (*Mother, The End of St. Petersburg*) and of Dovzhenko (*Earth, Arsenal*). A controversy over the radical orientation of Eisenstein's work occasioned a liberal statement on censorship from Malraux in May 1927, to be followed more concretely in 1959, when he was minister of culture, by his rejection of official precensorship tactics.

Since the golden age of the Ballets Russes in Paris with the impresario Diaghilev, the dancer Nijinsky, and Cocteau and Stravinsky in the wings, the French aesthetes looked more and more to Russia for cultural inspiration. During the Popular Front in France in the 1930s support would also come from this highly politicized part of the world. The attendance of Malraux and his French colleagues at the Writers' Congress in Moscow in 1934 reflected a flirtation with Soviet literature. Malraux's address on social realism entitled "L'Art est une conquête," came across as an extern's critical view of Soviet literature at the time. This had less of a startling effect upon the Russians or Communist sympathizers than did André Gide's deflating *Retour de l'URSS*.

During his stay in Moscow Malraux met with Eisenstein to plan the filming of the 1933 classic novel *La Condition humaine*, a formidable challenge. For their collaboration, Malraux provided a synopsis and part of the scenario with key images sketched out, but he would write the dialogues later. The final technical script would be in the hands of Eisenstein, for Malraux was not about to tell a man of genius how to create his work of art. Because of political harassment and other complications, Eisenstein was unable to make the film, just as Meyerhold was prevented from staging a dramatized version of *La Condition humaine* as planned. James Agee's attempt to write a scenario also evaporated in 1939. Fred Zinnemann's 1969 production with a screenplay first intended by Jean Cau and then later Han Suyin was underway when MGM pulled out its multimillion-dollar support. The film would have to wait until 1979 for a production to be initiated, based on the script by Suyin. In the fall of 1979, Costa-Gavras signed a contract to film the classic.

Well before the outbreak of the Civil War in Spain, Malraux struggled against Fascist tendencies both in the colonialist mentality of French Indochina and in Hitler's cancerous influence in Germany. Malraux's novel *Le Temps du mépris* (1935) announced Fascism's impending entry onto center stage, and his trip to Spain in May 1936 revealed the imminent danger of the coming conflict. He was like a seismograph indicating earthshaking castastrophes in Indochina, China, Germany, and now Spain. In the country of Goya scarred by political and religious turmoil, Malraux observed that the influence of the Popular Front offered a note of hope that this "revolutionary" would underline in his reconstruction of the Spanish scene during his address in Marseilles in May 1936, recorded by *Le Petit Provençal* and *Le Petit Marseillais*. He saw the masses in Spain growing in strength, flexing their collective muscles. In *Regards*, the illustrated weekly of the Popular Front, Malraux accentuated the necessity of the union of art and the movement of the masses, dominated by the evolution of new techniques in mass media. He asserted that, above all, the quality of collective art must be ensured that the maximum of conscience/consciousness (in the intellectual and moral sense of the word) will be given it.[7] Already the preliminaries of his aesthetic theory of cinema can be discerned, coming to fruition shortly in his own filmmaking as well as meditation on film, *L'Esquisse d'une psychologie du cinéma*.

Less than two months following Malraux's return from Spain, General Francisco Franco took action. From the Canary Islands where he prepared his troops, Franco began the move toward Madrid, the *coeur rouge* of Spain, on 18 July 1936, hoping to restore law and order in the carnival atmosphere of the Communist-oriented, though legitimately established government. Two days later, it appears that Malraux the adventurer was en route for Spain to stave off any further Fascist growth.

Discussing Malraux's film work during this period of the war between wars without presenting his sense of *engagement* would be like attempting to decipher Cocteau's cinema world without understanding his notion of poetry. Malraux's commitment to the Republican or Loyalist cause in Spain would be extensive. His first major involvement would be with the International Air Squadron, which he helped organize and direct. Since most of the army materiel and officials went with Franco in the political and military schism, the Republicans would be in need of leaders and equipment, not to mention discipline and unity. Malraux tried to provide for the Loyalists in the best way possible, as he solicited planes to replace the old Republican models. The initial major military engagement for the Air Squadron would be in mid-August 1936. This was still the moment of Malraux's "illusion lyrique," a time when hope still flourished among the Loyalists, as the novelist said in Jorge Semprun's film *Les Deux Mémoires*, a time when a sector of the Spanish people saw Fascism arriving and staunchly rejected it. Malraux described this first year of struggle as a transformation from the fundamental disorder of the Republicans to a veritable structure that had the power to confront the phalanx of the organized enemies.[8] At this point he was already in the heart of the action.

Early December 1936 found Malraux in Geneva soliciting aircraft for his squadron. An international embargo was established much to the disadvantage of the Republicans, since outside of Germany and Italy's backing of Franco, the foreign powers, fearing a disruption of peace in their own countries, showed a reluctance to offer support to either side of this fraternal strife.

On 27 December 1936, in that first year of the war, a particular incident occurred that would supply the cornerstone for Malraux's novel, film, and propaganda speeches. Malraux's orders were to attack Teruel and the road to Saragossa with at least two bombers. At the last moment his plane was unable to participate in the mission. The other aircraft succeeded in the operation but unfortunately crashed in the mountains. Malraux immediately organized his crew and the local populace to bring them down. This personal experience served as a prism through which Malraux's imagination would pass in order to create a multicolored image in new aesthetic forms.

As the limited force of the Air Squadron gradually crumbled for want of equipment in early 1937, Malraux undertook his second mission as propagandist on behalf of the Republican government. He toured the nonintervening countries of the United States, France, and Canada to seek medical and financial support for the Loyalists. Malraux, a representative of the Alliance of Intellectual Anti-Fascists, made his way from one university milieu to another—Princeton, Harvard, Columbia, and so on. In Hollywood, visiting with some of the leading actors and directors at the time, he first thought of making a film on the Spanish Civil War, which would eventually be a prolongation of his propaganda tour. Following his American odyssey, Malraux traveled to Canada in early April 1937, where he spoke to students at McGill University and members of the League Against Fascism. The propagandist then returned to France and would soon again be in embattled Spain. The days of preaching for the Republic dissolved into images of the front.

Before making his own film to interpret the controversial events of the first year of the war, Malraux was already familiar with the militant filmmaker Joris Ivens' film, *The Spanish Earth*, sponsored by the Contemporary Historians, Inc.—Lillian Hellman, Frederick March, Louise Rainer, John Dos Passos, Archibald MacLeish and Ernest Hemingway. Several years earlier Malraux had thought of Ivens as a possible director for filming *La Condition humaine* and then Dovzhenko before he eventually settled on Eisenstein.

While members of the Contemporary Historians, Inc. were realizing their goal of portraying the initial events of the war,[9] Malraux undertook his third gesture of Republican support. His novel *L'Espoir*, an optimistic, philosophical fresco filled with cinematic images of the situation in Spain from 18 July 1936 to 18 March 1937 and containing more than fifty characters, was completed in November 1937 and published in December by Gallimard. In the meantime, Franco's military stranglehold was suffocating the Republicans.

With the war already into its second year, Malraux initiated plans for a pro-Republican film. When presented with the funds from the propaganda tour through the United States and Canada, Juan Negrín, president of the Council, volunteered his support to any of the projects that Malraux proposed in favor of the Spanish Republic. Now came the time for the president of the Council to hold to his word. José Bergamín introduced Malraux to influential members of the Department of Public Instruction. The Loyalist government then proposed a budget equivalent to $90,000,the necessary photographic film, and priority assistance from the various branches of the government. Max Aub in his scenario said that Malraux had 1,800 American theaters assured him for exhibiting the film with an average of 2,000 spectators per day per theater. These figures may be a bit optimistic considering that the subject of the Spanish Civil War was hotly controversial in this anti-Communist country and that the American public had never gotten accustomed to subtitles, a fact proved later when *Espoir* was shown in February 1947 in New York.

Despite his many encounters with the cinema world, the Malraux of 1938 had no technical experience and was thus obliged to rely upon the various skills of his crew. The playwright Max Aub and the critic Denis Marion[10] served as assistants facilitating the elaborate operation. On the recommendation of Jacques Prévert, Louis Page was selected for the photography with aid from André Thomas and Manuel Berenguer. Boris Peskine provided the script, and the major responsibility for the selection of actors fell to Max Aub. In June 1938, he auditioned vaudeville stars as well as local farmers and villagers when he went about choosing the sites in and around Barcelona with the approval of Malraux.

For pragmatic reasons the film would be made in Spanish with subtitles prepared for each country of distribution. One of the first titles proposed was *Sang de Gauche*, which evolved to *Sierra de Teruel*, *L'Espoir*, and then finally *Espoir*. According to the original plan of Malraux and Aub, the film would have forty sequences describing the harmonious cooperation of the air corps, guerrillas, and the peasants. Filming began in early August 1938, at the Orfea Studio of Barcelona, but not without incident. Lack of materials for the sets, interruptions of electrical current for the developing process, scarcity of quality film, technical problems with the sound truck, and obstacles created by the unions all made for an onerous task.

From August 1938 to January 1939, the "Producción Malraux" overcame one challenge after another in the filming of the mock-up plane designed by Bloch or the scenes in the cable car near Montserrat, the staging of the car and cannon crash or the choreographing of the funeral cortège. The ultimate problem arose when Malraux and company were forced to leave Barcelona on 23-24 January 1939, a day prior to Franco's penetration into the Catalan bastion. The film was incomplete, lacking twenty-two of the originally planned sequences, and scarred technically with rough edges. Once back in Paris, George Grace and Malraux attempted to make a coherent document of the work, filling in the gaps with aerial shots from the stock of the Cinémathèque française and with scenes shot in a village in southwestern France that resembled the original Spanish sites. Darius Milhaud composed the accompanying music for the eleven-minute segment of the cortège in its serpentlike descent from the mountain inspired in part by Tintoretto and Eisenstein. Approximately 2,500 Republican troops and sympathizers from the local village participated in order to capture this heroic gesture of fraternity that Malraux actually experienced in December 1936, in Teruel.

The narrative in essence is unpretentious: Following a simple eulogy by Commander Peña for the dead aviator Rivelli and a brief guerrilla action in the streets, a peasant crosses the Franquist lines to report the location of a Fascist encampment. Two planes bomb the airfield. One is struck, however, and crashes into the mountainside, resulting in the famous "descente de la montagne" of the dead and wounded avaitors. To show the correlation of the novel *L'Espoir* and the film *Espoir* or *Sierra de Teruel*, we can schematize the relationship of the various sequences completed with the corresponding pagination from the novel:[11]

Film Sequence	Action	*L'Espoir* (Pléiade Ed.)
I	1937: Marcelino Rivelli's death resulting from the crash of the Republican plane.	pp. 568-69
II	The eulogy of the dead pilot by Peña, Commander of the International Air Squadron.	p. 497
III	The plan of Peña and the pilot Muñoz to bomb a strategic bridge.	pp. 785-86
IV	A distribution of arms among the guerrillas.	pp. 443; 541; 627; 734; 771; 781
V	The peasant José's report of the Fascist airfield to the authorities of the Popular Front.	pp. 630; 808
VI	Guerrilla action in the streets.	pp. 446-47
VII	The suicide attack of the Republican car into the Fascist cannon.	pp. 453-54
VIII	A gathering of the local Popular Front to procure containers for dynamiting.	(no parallel in the novel)
IX	The collection of materials for the dynamiting mission.	(no parallel in the novel)
X	The plane crash of the former German pilot Schreiner during a political discussion of the members of the International Air Squadron.	pp. 491-94
XI	Schreiner's successful attempt at antiaircraft machine-gunning.	p. 500
XII	The crossing of the Franquist lines by the peasant José and his guide Pío.	p. 808
XIII	José's arrival at Peña's headquarters followed by preparations to bomb the airfield and the bridge.	pp. 808-10
XIV	The requisitioning of cars to illuminate the Republican airfield.	pp. 810-12
XV	The takeoff of the two Republican aircraft.	pp. 813-15
XVI	The bombing of the enemy airfield and bridge, resulting in a crash of one of the planes into the mountainside.	pp. 816-23

XVII	Peña's preparatory measures for the descent of the dead and wounded airmen.	pp. 823-27
XVIII	The epic cortège accompanying the heroic Republicans into the village, with Darius Milhaud's lyrical *Cortège funèbre* setting the tone.	pp. 827-37

Except for a few minor sequences, much of the material was already present in the third part of the novel, called "Les Paysans." Yet the film could not be considered an adaptation of the literary work. Denis Marion clarifies the question of a possible adaptation of the novel in this manner:

> /.../ André Malraux had never planned on adapting his novel for the screen; his intention was rather to compose an original scenario that was based on the same material. He created this scenario working from three kinds of sources: events that he had personally experienced (such as the airplane raid), events related to him by those who acted them out in his film (such as the receptacles for dynamite), and events taken from his own imagination (such as the passage through the lines). He did his utmost to give them a visually striking form while strictly preserving their credibility.[12]

The forty-eight-hour period covered by the film is a telescoping of events of the novel that occur between 18 July 1936 and 18 March 1937. Malraux in a sense cast himself into the characters of Manuel and Peña in the novel, and Peña in the film. His air corps participated in the bombing mission and he, like Peña, manifested great concern for his wounded men following the plane crash. The character José, who plays a dramatic role in the events leading up to the bombing of the Fascist site, could have been inspired by the Olmedo peasant who crossed the enemy lines with much danger to his life, as reported in *Le Temps* for 3 September 1936. It was the same peasant who deeply impressed Bertolt Brecht when the playwright saw *Espoir* on 27 March 1947 in the United States. Brecht referred to the acting of this peasant who could not recognize his own countryside from the bomber as magnificent.[13] The essence of the descent, for example, was vividly described, in a style befitting the tale-tellers Giono and Pagnol, by Malraux at Harvard in March 1937:

> On December 27th (1936), one of the planes in my squadron was brought down in the region of Teruel—inside our lines. It crashed down in a high mountainous place, 2,000 meters above sea level. Snow was falling. In this region there are few villages. It was only after some

hours that peasants arrived and began to make stretchers for the wounded and a coffin for the dead.

When all was ready the descent began. There were no roads, only mule trails. The old peasant women—almost all of them have sons in the militia—had decided to accompany the wounded. But when the time came not they alone but the whole village followed us in single file down the narrow mountain path. At each village along the way the people were waiting; and each village, when the wounded had passed by, was emptied of its inhabitants. When we reached the first large settlement in the valley, there, too, the people stood waiting before the low walls of the Spanish town. They gazed in silence at the first wounded, those wounded in the legs. They were used to such things. But when those who had been wounded in the face were carried past, men with flat bandages where their noses should have been, their leather tunics still covered with coagulated blood—then the women and children began to cry. I raised my eyes: the file of peasants extended now from the height of the mountain to its base. This was the grandest image of fraternity I have ever encountered in my life; those abandoned villages, that entire people following men wounded for their sake, men whom they had never seen before, descending like an antique procession, while their sobs, mounting in the great silence of the gorge, made a sound like the roar of an underground river.

At the same moment the fascist aviators who had been wounded that very day were given a military escort. And I could not help thinking that every one of these men lying on the stretchers made by the hands of peasants, had been willing to risk his life in the specific hope that no military escort, but the strong fraternity of the people themselves, would henceforth accompany those who fight for their ideas.[14]

In this way, Malraux took the ingredients of his lived experience and colored them in a dramatic fashion in his propaganda speeches, as well as in his literary and cinematic work.

From the point of view of technique, the rhythm of the film is slow and syncopated, and the action is difficult to follow, owing in great part to the sequences that were not filmed, as well as the poor sound equipment. In many instances the dialogues are inaudible or artificial-sounding as a result of the inexperience of the peasants or the vaudeville background of the principal actors. The action, however, often appears realistic, with some shots of the tanks and planes emanating from the documentary footage of the Cinémathèque. *The Spanish Earth* of Joris Ivens would bear a greater sense of realism since it was filmed on location during the battle scenes, whereas *Espoir* was made in Barcelona, Collbató, and Tarragona with reconstructed scenes, such as those dealing with the guerrillas or the aviators. It was because of the filming of certain scenes as these that the American audiences of the 1940s felt that they were watching actual documentary footage from the war.

Malraux, like Marguerite Duras, would readily admit that he was not a cinéaste with technical skills, but he could compensate for this deficiency by his visual imagination and his ability to effectively narrate an incident.[15] He was a true aesthete who had seen the relationship of literature and film both in style and content since the 1920s. The international press of 1939, 1946, 1970, and 1976, underscores the *beauté plastique* of Malraux's film, especially the night scenes and several striking images that recur throughout the work. The flight of pigeons juxtaposed with the car crashing into the Fascist cannon and the shot of the sunflowers flowing in the breeze after Pío is shot reflect the same depth as that found in Eisenstein's imagery. The collision with rapid cutting and the descent from the mountain in slowcutting stand out as excellent examples of the dramatic use of montage in the crescendo of images. The latter sequence, an orchestration of at least sixty-two shots filmed separately for the most part and then meticulously assembled by Malraux and Grace, has often been compared to the "Odessa Steps" sequence of *Potemkin.* The first shot of this cinematic movement is said to have been inspired by Mantegna's *Descent from the Cross* and the final one from Tintoretto's double movement in *Ascent to Calvary*. The powerful images of death, human love, and the sacred blend finally into a collective Spanish *Pietà*.

Espoir was aesthetically well conceived and effected, although it was deliberately directed toward persuading an audience to side with the Republican forces. Once engaged in the cause, Malraux was successfully integrated into the propaganda program of the Ministry of Information where all possible means were utilized to sway the Franquist sympathizers (bourgeois, rightists, Catholic hierarchy, and the like) to favor the Republicans, as well as to boost the latter's slumping morale. The radio of both camps, the colorful, instructive and encouraging posters, Russian revolutionary films projected by Ilya Ehrenburg and Louis Aragon, the gamut of the press in its attitude of commitment to the cause, the guerrilla theater of Lorca and Aub—all were used in psychological warfare with greater and greater technological skill and aesthetic sense. In *Espoir* the propaganda elements are present side by side with artistic images. It would be advantageous to distinguish between the propagandistic and aesthetic tendencies of *Espoir*—a Gordian knot, however, that may never be cut through entirely.

In art and literature, propaganda—the deliberate manipulation either intellectually or emotionally of an audience—is a common, and almost reputable phenomenon. Pablo Picasso, Bertolt Brecht, and Louis-Ferdinand Céline channeled their respective publics to feel and think in a certain manner. In film, Leni Riefenstahl, Sergei Eisenstein, and Robert Flaherty at one moment or other graphically sponsored some organization or event.[16] Malraux, appealing to the whole man, would also utilize this psychological force of the medium to help break the arms embargo against the Spanish republic. All his financial and artistic means were employed in presenting characters and actions with which the spectator could identify.

Certain factors were already in Malraux's favor. His reputation as an established novelist and recipient of the Prix Goncourt for *La Condition humaine* in 1933 would be a highly attractive element in his propaganda ventures. In certain circles the anti-Fascist and leftist tendencies of this political figure would be positively singled out, as in the French, American, and Canadian press. From his propaganda tour Malraux knew his audiences and was aware of which themes to accentuate or avoid. Subtlety would be primary in his film work as it was in his other aesthetic expressions, and he sculptured the content of the work in a concrete yet universal form.

The individual and collective support of the Republican cause in all its facets forms the very nucleus of the film. Those who are killed for it—Carral, Rivelli, Pío, and Saïdi—have died for a noble reason, the amelioration of the human condition. The specter of death raises no fear in the hearts of the combatants. In the novel *L'Espoir* the remark is callously made that these heroes perversely preferred mankind to family, but in the minds of those accepting the risk of death, they could not avoid helping their family when struggling in the name of humanity. In Malraux's address at Harvard, as well as in Edouard Corniglion-Molinier's original preface to the film, the dominant motif is the preservation of human and universal values at all costs. The poverty-stricken villagers donate some of their last household receptacles to assist the dynamiting mission, and their vehicles to aid in illuminating the airfield. The International Air Squadron—with a German, the son of a Belgian Fascist leader, an Arab, and an Italian in the ranks of the Republicans, all of different political persuasions—reveals the dimension and consequence of this war. The squadron members have come from all parts of the world to combat Fascism, as Denis Marion states in the first of the series of titles throughout the film. The film concludes with the most profound tribute to the collective support of the cause, as Malraux photographs the 2,500 army recruits and the peasants of the outlying villages. The government's release of this number of able men at such a crucial moment in the course of the war indicates the significance of this film in the propaganda program.

Another major motif evident in the propaganda speeches and in the films was that of the poverty of the Republicans. For socio-economic reasons they received a poor education to which José is a witness, for he is unable to read or write. A woman who approaches Captain Peña during the descent says she made the bouillon from the *last* chicken in the village. So tragic was the situation of hunger that stray cats and dogs would often disappear from the streets to be found in the stew pots of the villagers, as Max Aub recounted to us in a conversation in 1971. With a few antiquated rifles and airplanes the Republicans were ill-equipped compared to the technologically advanced troops of Franco's reinforcements from Germany and Italy. The Republicans were certainly the underdogs in the conflict, and Malraux wished to make this factor evident to the international public.

The theme of maternity appears in the final segment of *Espoir* as the elderly woman offers help to the badly wounded Muñoz, for she, too, has a son at the front. *Fraternité virile*, the keystone of many of Malraux's works, becomes apparent in the barracks scene and the meetings of the Popular Front, as well as the last sequence of the funeral procession. The descent rivals Leni Riefenstahl's *Triumph of the Will*, which exhibits the same need for togetherness in building an esprit de corps, and the propaganda film *Für Uns*, which strikes a universal note of pathos in the cult of the heroic dead.

Malraux's intention was to integrate these themes into a dramatic narrative filled with several levels of action. As if in a symphonic arrangement, the themes are introduced naturally, carefully developed and repeated throughout the work, and then recapitulated in the last tragic moments. The presentation of the diverse motifs is far from being a polemic or overbearing statement. For instance, there is no harshness toward Franco, Hitler, or Mussolini, who are simply a part of the almost faceless, collective enemy, the embattled foe of all mankind, according to Malraux.

Certain cinematic themes are directed specifically toward the Spanish Republican situation, whereas others exhibit a more universal dimension, aimed at helping in the progress of humanity. Just as in the Indochina of the 1920s, Malraux's ideal was to restore social justice to a divided land where the poor and unlearned were prey to overpowering traditional forces. In this film, written in the *futur antérieur*, Malraux seems to say that the men of Teruel in December 1937 and the women and children of Guernica on that fateful market day of 26 April 1937 did not die in vain.[17] They are martyrs in a cause greater than themselves, which would only temporarily end with the conclusion of this war. In our historical perspective, it can be seen as just the rehearsal, and Act One of a new bloody drama would begin in September 1939. Meanwhile, Adolf Hitler, the director of this gruesome theater, would congratulate his actors:

> My comrades: At last once again I am able to salute you personally. I am extremely pleased to see you here before me, and above all, I am

very proud of you. The entire German people greet you with a spirit of joy and pride, and certainly they are not wrong in expressing their emotion. We gratefully acknowledge those who, as soldiers, had to sacrifice their bodies, their lives, their health in the service of such a mission. We finally thank the families of the fallen dead who today weep over the victims, their courageous husbands and sons. These men have fallen, but their death and their suffering will in the future give life to an infinity of other lives in Germany.

Legionnaires and soldiers, long live the German people! Long live the Spanish people and their leader Franco! Long live the Italian people and their Duce! People of Germany, long live our Legion! Sieg Heil![18]

Edouard Corniglion-Molinier's preface to the film could serve as a reply to Hitler's homage to the Condor Legion, which was responsible for the bombing of Guernica, as the producer emphasizes the human and the universal and not the national:

It was in the spirit of conscientious love that we went to Spain and made this film on the Civil War. It tells the story of Man in his misery, yet with his great desire to live his life without humiliation and to ask for nothing save the simple privilege of being a man—something which cruel Fate all too often denies him.

We have tried, therefore, to be human rather than social, in a film such as this where "plastic beauty" has such importance. An ill-suited vocabulary, whose subtle influence frequently escapes our notice, inspires many of our contemporaries to utter words of hate.

This film is meant to show how Man's generosity in a fleeting struggle can benefit the Man of the future. The Man of the present will pass away, yet this struggle of his on earth is with more enduring elements than himself—elements which join in the fight and yet do not pass away.[19]

Malraux's propaganda efforts in making *Espoir* would, nonetheless, be in vain. Once the film was edited in Paris, it was scheduled for commercial release in September, 1939. The signing of the Germano-Soviet non-aggression pact and the opening salvos of the war obliged the French government of Edouard Daladier to hold off permission for commercial distribution of the film. *Espoir* would not be projected publicly until after the war, following the Gestapo's unsuccessful attempt to destroy the film, just as the Nazis wished to do with Ivens' *Spanish Earth*.[20]

The film, made into an anti-Fascist document with the introduction by the Minister of Foreign Affairs Maurice Schumann, won the Louis Delluc Prize in 1946 and would soon become a favorite among Malraux cultists. With Rossif's *Mourir à Madrid* and Ivens' *Spanish Earth*, Malraux's *Espoir* would rank as one of the most significant and popular among the approximately 500 films—long, short, fiction, and documentary—made on the subject of the Spanish Civil War.[21]

What follows in Malraux's life with regard to cinema almost appears anticlimatic, yet it shows at least a growing concern for the quality of film standards. From his experiences in filming in 1938-39 and from his other artistic and literary interests, Malraux wrote *Esquisse d'une psychologie du cinéma* in 1939 and later published it in the wake of the war. This sketch, a type of meditation, charts the evolution of cinema from the image of art to a moving film. Parts Three and Four—Malraux's discussion of the transformation of the silent into the sound film—have a particular bearing on the relationship of literature and cinema, for here the artist confronts the issue of the staged play with the dialogue assured and the length of material convenient, something obvious in the films of Pagnol, Guitry, and even Duras in the case of *Des Journées entières dans les arbres*. At a time when sound was not yet a decade old in Europe, the novelist/cinéaste lamented the fact that the direction of sound filmmakers regressed when they resorted to filming stage plays.

During the Cannes Film Festival in 1959, Malraux, the minister of culture at the time, again voiced his impressions of the importance of cinema as a means of international communication, in which national barriers disappear as people the world over dream the same dreams under the same star-filled sky.[22] In this notion of film as a *collective dream*, Malraux underscored the *collective* and Cocteau the *dream*, as we have already observed. As a government official in 1959, Malraux also promised that he would not precensor a film by judging the script alone, as was done, for example, with several projects of Eisenstein. The film must rise or fall on its fully realized form, on its own merits.

Throughout his life, Malraux saw the powerful force that cinema could be, vis-à-vis the masses. Marcel Martin eulogized Malraux as an *artiste engagé* in referring to *Espoir* as a masterpiece, "a perfect balance between the *end* (a humanitarian and revolutionary message) and the *means* (a style based on a dialectic of audiovisual relationships)."[23] In this one film where the novelist/cinéaste goes from the physical to the metaphysical, and from the political to the cosmic, there is a valiant attempt to harness the medium and to create an aesthetic piece of propaganda that would aid the Loyalists. The Republican cause has been swallowed up into man's history, but *Espoir* remains a document that will preserve Malraux's cinematic genius and dedicated struggle for the sake of justice.

Malraux: ***Espoir*****, 1939.**

Malraux: *Espoir*, **1939.**

Malraux: *Espoir*, **1939.**

Malraux: *Espoir*, **1939.**

6

ALAIN ROBBE-GRILLET

In all my fictional works, either novels or films, there exists a certain number of irreconcilable organizing elements which establish or attempt to establish some order in the ensemble of the narrative.

—Colloque de Cerisy (29 June-8 July 1975)

Destiny appears to have labored overtime with Alain Robbe-Grillet. It enticed him to leave his comfortable "clan fermé" of Paris' fourteenth arrondissement for a more tropical climate in order to "care for sick banana trees," as he once referred to his first profession of agricultural engineer. The allure continued as he felt enticed to write his iconoclastic novels that were immediately condemned to the cellars of the Editions de Minuit. In Italy, and especially in the United States where he occasionally held forth in the sacred academic realm of New York University, he soon became "the Pope of the New Novel." His pontifical reign would frequently be interrupted as destiny finally led him to the celluloid cult where he would be demoted by critics from pope or high priest to simple erotic "choirboy of cinema." His career in cinema, checkered by one controversy after another, comprises six films, two *ciné-romans* (one of which is a technical script), and a *Continuité dialoguée.*

The average frequenter of the world of illusion, intrigued by films infused with exciting narrative, some psychological meaning, and solid character development, is not readily recompensed in viewing a Robbe-

Grillet film. Instead, the viewer tends to encounter in the cinéaste's works an enigmatic and abstruse universe filmed in a cerebral, philosophical, and literary vein. Designed for the already initiated, each work allows for a plethora of radical interpretations. Certain of his films, for example the highly convoluted *L'Homme qui ment*, would make the oracle of Delphi appear as clear as crystal. More concerned with form than with content the director purposefully obfuscates his materials, teasing his audience and offering them humorous but recherché anecdotes in one aesthetic parody/paradox after another. The effect at times alternates between hypnosis and ennui, depending upon the spectator's background and expectations.

Although Robbe-Grillet had been a longtime admirer of Eisenstein and Lang (and later Godard), his debut in the cinema formally dates only to 1959.[1] Pursuing the suggestion of Samy Halfon who later produced other films of Robbe-Grillet, the author planned to direct the film *L'Immortelle,* but unfortunate financial problems forced its postponement. In the meantime, Pierre Courau and Raymond Froment were looking for a screenwriter who could work as effectively with Resnais as did Marguerite Duras when she furnished the script for *Hiroshima, mon amour.* Robbe-Grillet immediately expressed some interest in this type of collaboration. He already saw in the previous works of Resnais reflections of a theatrical, operatic, or statuary ambiance that were very similar to his own aesthetic conceptions. After their first encounter, Robbe-Grillet and Resnais decided to undertake a collective work. The following week, Robbe-Grillet submitted four scenarios to the film director who expressed a willingness to film all four as well as two of the author's novels—*La Jalousie* and perhaps *Dans le labyrinthe* or *Les Gommes.* A short time later Robbe-Grillet supplied Resnais with a technical script for *L'Année dernière à Marienbad,* which the author would eventually publish as a *ciné-roman.*[2]

Riding on the crest of *Marienbad's* success, Robbe-Grillet was assisted by Samy Halfon in procuring the necessary funds for the original *L'Immortelle* to be filmed as a Franco-Italian co-production. This film of a mysterious encounter, disappearance, and quest in Istanbul was completed in 1963 and earned for the director the celebrated Prix Louis Delluc, just as *Espoir* gained the Prix for Malraux in 1946. Pushing his avant-garde techniques further, Robbe-Grillet, in 1966, made *Trans-Europ-Express,* a film within a film dealing with dope smuggling on the luxurious TEE from Paris to Amsterdam via Antwerp. Two years later, through some contacts in Czechoslovakia, he was able to film *L'Homme qui ment,* depicting a certain Boris Varissa's reconstruction of his association with the resistance fighter Jean Robin. A parallel with the Polish filmmaker Tadeusz Konwicki's political surrealist parable, *Salto,* is striking.

Robbe-Grillet directed his first color film, *L'Eden et après,* in 1970 with a counterpart for French television called *N a pris les dés*, a film that was not programmed by the ORTF until 1975. In Eden, the games and reveries of a university student, Violette, remove her from the boredom of her intellectual pursuits. Robbe-Grillet then directed two films back-to-back in 1974, both works drawing myriad negative reactions: *Glissements progressifs du plaisir,* inspired by Michelet's *La Sorcière,* which Robbe-Grillet encountered in Barthes's *Michelet par lui-même,* and *Le Jeu avec le feu,* where the *feu* is the taboo subject of incest.

All of these films, based on Robbe-Grillet's personal grasp of a contemporary "mythology," have to be approached differently from other classical or commercial films. They must be faced with an openness toward multiple interpretations, recalling Resnais's remark that *Marienbad* itself is a film open to many myths.[3] Each of Robbe-Grillet's cinematic works is directed more toward the senses than the intellect, despite the fact that such films as *Glissements* contain a multitude of anecdotal references to Michelet, Bataille, de Sade, and the surrealists. Furthermore each of Robbe-Grillet's films is constructed as a visual odyssey in sound, not a psychological exposition of a "story." Hence, entering into contact with Robbe-Grillet's film repertoire, the spectator must not expect the traditional form or content common to any commercial film but must first learn to *experience* without preconceptions. To illustrate this point, Robbe-Grillet emphasized on the interview panel of the "Radioscopie" program of France Culture (7 February 1977) that after the first viewing of *Le Jeu avec le feu,* the spectator "does not *understand* anything, but simply *sees* and *hears;* it is not necessary to understand." It is therefore more important to trust one's instinct than intellect in confronting a Robbe-Grillet film, a different approach from the one that the viewer must take to a political film of Malraux or a filmed play of Pagnol or Guitry. Marguerite Duras later took this tendency of Robbe-Grillet one step further.

The task at hand is to examine the component parts of the director's cinematic creation, to penetrate his psychology of the cinema (to borrow Malraux's phraseology), and thus to grasp his originality. In confronting the structural aspect of his films—most difficult to "comprehend" at times—one has to come to grips with the narrative language, the characterization, the decor, and the sound track. Secondary to this is his thematic development, a preoccupation with certain images that remain constant in his work, such as the labyrinth, the game with overtones of ritual and chance, images of doubles, blood, and finally a full gamut of experiences from the exotic and esoteric to the erotic.

Structural Dimension

Similar to an intricately structured sentence, a film of Robbe-Grillet has to be "parsed" to gain fuller consciousness of its grammatical ingredients and their rapport with each other. This would certainly distress Robbe-Grillet, for he senses that many critics, including Roland Barthes, the early high priest of the Nouveau Roman criticism, too facilely project their own philosophies into an author's work. Before engaging ourselves nonetheless in this type of adventure in cinematic language, we must go back one step to the director's origins with language in his literary works. Although Robbe-Grillet hesitates to make the rapport of the cinema with literature, given the uniqueness of each genre, a similarity of "attitudes" common to the New Novel and the avant-garde or experimental cinema of Robbe-Grillet can still be detected. In both, there is a primacy of form over content, to use traditional language, as well as a disrupted or illogical narrative with no visible sense at times. Both reader and filmgoer alike can also discover in the two forms of expression a neutral, occasionally shifting perspective, one-dimensional characterization (almost never psychological), and a geometric placement of persons and objects. Throughout the films and the novels, there is a minimum or perhaps even an absence of linear, chronological development. In a certain sense, then, we can assume that Robbe-Grillet has entered into the domain of cinema with at least some part of his literary heritage, but where he "says" in his novels, he "shows" in his films, the author/filmmaker remarked on occasion.

With all cinematic undertakings there occurs some type of relationship (conscious or unconscious) of the director with his public. Robbe-Grillet in his films goes one step further, inviting his public to participate in the film itself. In the case of *TEE,* the viewer is encouraged not only to *participate* but to *invent,* along with the actors and film crew, the possible directions the film will take. This is an alluring invitation for the frustrated filmmaker in the *cinéphile.* Contrasting his work with the closed world of Balzac, the director thus solicits the spectator's cooperation: "The work which I am proposing to you is, on the contrary, an appeal to your creative participation; each of you in a sense must make the film."[4] His detailed introduction to *Marienbad* also requests the same type of creative contribution or permanent creativity. The structure of the film never remains definitive, but is totally open, in flux, and perpetually in an "état naissant," a continuous state of being born, to make use of Robbe-Grillet's own imagery.[5]

In a critique of *Marienbad,* Penelope Houston succinctly resumes this type of collaborative experience:

> No picture could be more fully realized, less of a do-it-yourself kit for filmgoers, than *L'Année Dernière;* but it is a film which opens up perspectives, alternatives, and at the same time that it spreads them out before the filmgoer it also contains them. Think of a solution, and the film will probably have forestalled you; the meanings will be there, the clues offered, yet when you get to what seems to be the centre of the maze, there's still another path, and another...[6]

Her perception of the film's openness and ambiguity reinforces the recurrent configuration of the labyrinth in Robbe-Grillet's films, beginning with the structure itself, especially obvious in such films as *L'Immortelle* and *L'Homme qui ment.*

In an unconventional fashion, the director attempts to create what he occasionally refers to as a "paysage intérieur," an interior or psychological landscape. In this intimate dimension, one must abandon all Cartesian principles, just as in an early cubist painting of Picasso or the "concrete music" of John Cage. It is the aesthetic feeling or experience that has more validity than the comprehension of the work.

First of all with respect to time, there is normally no linear or chronological progress in Robbe-Grillet's films. A dilation of time occurs, and all the action takes place in the present, often enough in the "mental present" of one of the characters. In *Marienbad* with all its Orphic nuances, deliberate or not, we never know if there was an already existent relationship between the seducer and the seduced, or if there was even a "last year." Despite a series of apparent flashbacks in *L'Homme*, one never fully realizes if Boris's past as recounted to his audience ever took place. With *L'Immortelle*, the different moments of the action may only exist in the mind of the French professor N, ruminating about the woman he loves, as the actor (N) and critic Jacques Doniol-Valcroze has recounted in his analysis of the film in *Cahiers du Cinéma.*[7]

Time as an organizing element in the narrative as well as a correlative of causality is also rejected by the cinéaste. We are uncertain if the actual events in the life of the young prostitute Alice in *Glissements*, accused of killing her companion Nora, occur simply in her imagination, more realistically in her past, or are merely hypotheses acted out in a vain effort to establish her innocence. Time thus has become relative.

A lack of logic also characterizes the films of Robbe-Grillet. In *TEE*, from a triple perspective, the hero Elias is filmed throwing a package into the water. One wonders if this is cubist repetition or refusal to choose the best shot. In any case, the repetitive act is not logical. Nor is the perpetual resurrection of Boris in *L'Homme qui ment* very rational. Alice, in *Glissements*, accidentally breaks the same bottle twice, "without any concern for continuity in the narrative," stipulates Robbe-Grillet in his *Continuité dialoguée* for the film.[8]

Often a fine line separates the zone of veracity from that of mendacity. Boris Varissa attempts to convice the public as well as the sister, wife, and maid of the Resistance fighter Jean Robin that he was a faithful companion to the latter during the war. He resumes his narrative several times, adapting it each time to his listener's expectations or interests. Here Boris leads us through a labyrinth of lies structured in a manner similar to *Glissements* where Alice offers several hypotheses to the crime; in the latter film, the viewer is literally left in the dark at the end, not knowing whether or not the voyeur really committed the first murder.

Reality—or at least what has been traditionally taken for reality—is fractured in every film of Robbe-Grillet. A vision or a waking dream—one is never certain. In *Marienbad* the action might perhaps be taking place in the mind of A or X. Violette in *Eden* goes off on a fantasy trip at the arrival of the stranger in the café. As noted earlier, the French professor of *L'Immortelle* could have imagined the series of events at a split second before his death, or perhaps as he reflected upon his relationship with his loved one. Did the lesbian and vampiric activity of Alice really take place in her past or was it only fantasized? One of the countless interpretations of *Marienbad*—diagnosed as everything from a metaphysical *Huis Clos* to an ultra-bourgeois mental hospital in the genre of Dr. Caligari—is that of a recurrent dream. This view is supported by the notion of disguise, displacement, condensation, and dramatization.[9] The event itself runs the gamut of possibilities: strategy, machination, trick, or genuine encounter. Freudian preoccupations of human sexuality and the Jungian overtones of the collective unconscious merge in this *photo-roman* of deliberate ambiguity. (Another illustrative example would be the chimerical *Jeu avec le feu*, a veritable reservoir of phantasms.)

Circular motion in film, which is not uncommon, is experienced when the conclusion of the work opens onto the beginning. Several of Robbe-Grillet's films utilize this type of movement. At the baroque hotel in *Marienbad*, for instance, A attends a performance of a play. The actress in the final act melodramatically says to her lover, "Je suis à vous," prefiguring A's attempt to leave the hotel with X at the film's closing. The entrance of the stranger into the Café Eden provokes an illusion. At the end of Violette's adventure, the stranger once again is seen entering the café. At the conclusion of *L'Homme*, Varissa gets up after being shot by Robin, and tells his story as he did earlier. At the end of *Glissements*, the inspector arrives at Alice's apartment as he did in the opening sequence, discovers the lawyer's body, and exclaims: "Alors, tout est à recommencer."[10] We are back where we started from—at the beginning.

The destruction of a "normal" narrative order through a juggling with time, causality, logic, and hypothesis has a certain bearing upon the content. The title *Glissements progressifs du plaisir*, according to the author, alludes to the gradual slipping into the realm of pleasure by the young prostitute Alice, as well as to the precipitation of the spectator into a state of uncertainty throughout the film because of its complicated style. The form and content of a film such as *Marienbad* cannot be separated, being so intimately related and manipulated to effect a total experience. In what is best referred to as a *mise-en-abîme* or work-within-a-work perspective, Robbe-Grillet has created with his *TEE* a film within a film, where suggestions, hypotheses, and instant replays all indicate a merging of form and content on both levels of the work.

When the director was questioned by his interviewer about the convoluted style that is so evident in his cinematic and literary opus, he simply remarked in a humorous fashion, that he is in agreement with Resnais's succinct quip: "Pourquoi faire simple, quand on peut faire compliqué?"[11] or in common parlance, "Why please the crowds when you can mesmerize them instead?"

The personages encountered in the disjointed narrative of Robbe-Grillet's films appear to be situated out of time and space. Theirs is a dehumanized world where they act out their entangled lives in a stylized reflection of the existential situation of contemporary man. This perspective is a manifestation of a larger sphere of contemporary literature and film where man—directionless, lost, and in anguish—confronts the absurd at every turn.

Among the characters in Robbe-Grillet's creations, the narrator plays a significant role. Alice, Elias, Boris, X, and N assume this function in one way or another. At certain times the camera takes their perspective, whereas at other times it becomes omniscient; hence, a fluctuation of views ensues that also has some relevance to the narrative structure discussed earlier.

As in his novels, the characters of Robbe-Grillet's films are most often nameless. For the sake of convenience they are given initials in the *ciné-roman*, for instance A, L, N, X, and M. Alice's name is never pronounced in *Glissements*. Such characters live apart from their nominal designation. The spectator has no idea from where these individuals come or where they are going; they only exist in our present. Boris, anonymous, walks through the microcosmic, Czechoslovakian village. The French professor is uprooted and set in an oriental ambiance of Istanbul. He is eternally lost in the labyrinth of his frustrating quest for L.

In a long litany of pejorative names, the critics of Robbe-Grillet have called these characters zombies, fossils, puppets, androids, robots, phantoms, or mannequins. Mute, frozen, sleek, or expressionless, they meander through uncertain intrigues. Jacques Doniol-Valcroze in *L'Immortelle* was told by the director to play the role of N with minimal facial expressions and hands dangling by his side, not unlike the cadaverous clientele of *Marienbad.* Violette and Alice appear in their respective films in a semicomatose state, especially as they involve themselves in the games or rituals. The stranger in *Eden* displays the cold, glassy stare and the same mysteriousness of Forsythe and Zinnemann's "Jackal." As the characters of Robbe-Grillet's novels, they are present, they stare, they record, and they narrate, eternally in their *maintenant.* It is life in its primordial state, nothing more, nothing less.

Some of these individuals confuse the identity of others. N, for example, is never certain who or what L represents. As for L, she remains enigmatic throughout *L'Immortelle*, speaking oriental languages and being tracked by a man in dark glasses with barking dogs. *TEE* abounds in deceptive identities, such as Eva the prostitute and double agent, surrounded by false spies and policemen. In *Eden*, after the stranger's death, he or his double reappears in Djerba. The waiter's name at the Café Eden is first given by Violette as Frantz, but then she says, "Most probably his name is not Frantz, but rather François Gervai, Daniel Dupont, Jean Robin, or whatever."[12] In the same film the name Duchemin becomes confused with Dutchman.

Since *L'Homme*, the last several films of Robbe-Grillet have been populated and even dominated by women, often beautiful, statuesque, and equally as frozen. Made in the image and likeness of A in *Marienbad*, they are usually exotic and give every indication at times of not being physically or psychologically present. Of greater import is how Robbe-Grillet applies their sundry powers. They play a key role in his notion of contemporary mythology and eroticism in particular, which is developed thematically at a later moment.

In this type of apparently dehumanized world, objects assume a more intense and dynamic function. There is a primacy of matter here that has been recognized in Robbe-Grillet's works from his earliest novels, this philosophy being referred to as *chosisme.* Such a perspective—labeled as a phenomenology, geometry, or topology of objects—shows things as they *are*, shorn of their relationships to humans. In their stark visual, spatial, and situational existence, they enhance the neutral world of humans.[13]

Images of a bottle, mannequin, shovel, and shoe recur ambiguously throughout *Glissements.* Here they become anecdotal; they have little or no reference to the major action, yet they intrigue the spectator since so much visual importance is given to them. Statues are highlighted in certain compositions in *TEE, Glissements,* and *L'Homme.* In *TEE*, a hollow book supposedly hides a revolver, but humorously enough, it is discovered to contain an ordinary razor. *Marienbad* reflects a sterile, fossilized world, harboring a plethora of objects that are utilized as "proofs" in the persuasion by X—the broken shoe, the picture with a winter scene, the statue of the couple, the photo taken "last year," and others. At times Robbe-Grillet assembles these objects as part of his thematic study of the labyrinth, as in the case of the storerooms in *Glissements* and *L'Homme*. With mirrors and windows, he adds to his treatment of duplicity and refraction of reality. Within each film, nonetheless, these objects in relationship to each other set up what may be considered as *rimes intérieures*, thus establishing a poetic network.

This digest of objects, circumscribed by emotionless personages, is captured with postcard precision, as indicated by Robbe-Grillet in his interviews and *ciné-romans*. In *L'Immortelle*, for example, he describes his location as "le bel Orient des cartes postales," somewhat similar to Stanley Kubrick's *Barry Lyndon* set within a northern climate. These compositions are to remain "eternal" and "more real" than the reality itself, according to Robbe-Grillet. As Carolina de Saxe—in *Le Jeu avec le feu*—opens various doors in the bizarre *maison de rendez-vous*, she comes across scenes of erotic rituals staged by the residents. In *Glissements*, the shots of the young girls about to be tortured are also posed and stereotyped, images that one associates with a popularized view of the Middle Ages. The barroom scene and the photographs of the statues in the garden in *Marienbad* seem to be taken from a postcard or photograph of the 1930's. The very photogenic L of *L'Immortelle* on the deck of a boat with Istanbul in the background could very well be a tourist's snapshot in a photo album.

Ordinarily Robbe-Grillet filmed on location for greater authenticity. For *L'Immortelle*, with a meticulous eye for composition, the director spent approximately two months in Istanbul isolating certain settings he would use in filming. The Tunisian village and surroundings of *Eden* were transposed into a study of blues and whites with the bleached sand and the azure sky. On occasion, the decor modified the scenario, as with *L'Homme* where it was also used as part of the psychology of the film. Discussing *L'Homme qui ment*, Gardies remarked that the physical decor with its lizard-covered walls and tree trunks in the forest poignantly enters into graphic opposition to the enigmatic tale-telling of Boris.[14]

In all of his films, Robbe-Grillet exhibits a highly developed sense of composition, making great demands upon his cameramen Igor Luther or Maurice Barry. The flow of images as a result creates a mesmerizing effect in *Eden*, or a feeling of existential *angst* with Boris in *L'Homme*. The poetics of imagery can thus be sensed profoundly, reinforced by the essential dimension of sound.

Right from his initiation with *Marienbad*, Robbe-Grillet has been concerned with correspondence of image and sound. For this film he preferred a jarring series of realistic and musical sounds excerpted from the daily life of a hotel. Resnais, however, chose the lugubrious organ music to serve as a background. With *L'Immortelle*, the elaborate score of Turkish music (classical, modern, sacred, and profane) and the harsh shrieking sounds of sirens, barking dogs, and the like accentuate the French teacher's sense of being lost. The unexpected in sound has a surrealistic air about it; as an apartment door in *Glissements* is opened, a melodious strain of Gregorian chant emerges. *Le Jeu avec le feu*, a "film opera," is a masterpiece of sound integration with excerpts from Verdi's *Il Trovatore* (strung end to end like a musical *calembour*, or play on words), the German military march *Erika*, and the Brazilian song "Carolina." At the Cerisy colloquium Robbe-Grillet underlined the fact that he never feels obliged to parallel a particular sound with its corresponding image. For this reason, perhaps, the cinéaste's critics and public whom he refers to as his "echo," are usually hopelessly *perdus*.

Michael Fano, the master of sound engineering for all of Robbe-Grillet's films, commented on the director's concern for absolute quality and precision in sound, observing that his films always richly display sound elements, as for example in *TEE* where the music of Verdi's operas were painstakingly interlaced with the image and action in their collaboration. The intricacies of the sound track of *L'Homme* reveal the careful, collective effort of Fano and Robbe-Grillet, resulting in a labyrinth of sound based on a series of twenty *formants,* or thematic structures. Supporting the specific thematic and structual components of this film, sound also has the power to convey the "lie": A glass falls and breaks, but nothing is heard.

Thematic Dimension

Despite its disjunctive nature, the structure of each of the director's films manoeuvres a content, or more accurately a series of themes, which is almost as challenging. His films manifest certain constants, recurrent imagery that can be traced through all of his films and most of his literary works. As one aspect of the content, this may be secondary to the form of expression that Robbe-Grillet has taken.

As mentioned previously, the mythology formulated by Robbe-Grillet originates in the complex, and at times "plastic," culture around him. From it he chooses certain representative expressions of diversified life-styles, preoccupations, and creeds. Hence, publicity, drugs, gangsters, ennui, and sex all provide him with ample material. It is significant to observe what the cinéaste does with these elements, which are also common to so many contemporary films.

The director views these elements as archetypes whose functions have been codified by society. He sets them out before the spectator sometimes in a humorous vein, and at other times apparently in a sympathetic fashion. Challenging or distorting them, he creates another usage and thus launches them into a new dimension. Many of these elements have become stereotypes, and Robbe-Grillet treats them as such, utilizing but criticizing them in their state of being "clichés." In the "Radioscopie" program Robbe-Grillet affirmed, "What I do is *manipulate* the stereotypes."

Interviewed by Michel Capdenac at the release of *TEE*, Robbe-Grillet elaborates upon his usage of these forms:

> Stereotypes nonetheless are living images of our world, images in which we live, which are also images of our unconscious. Whether designed to induce us to a vote or buy toothpaste, they still determine our actions. Philosophy today is in the street, shop windows, styles, and publicity. That is a fact, and it would be absurd to complain about it. The world in which I live is so, and that is that![15]

Many of these manifestations of our culture—labyrinthine forms, erotic objects, statuesque women, or intriguing rituals—form part of our collective unconscious, says Robbe-Grillet. Each civilization, be it Oriental or Occidental, consciously or unconsciously takes a basic construct, theme, or idea from its everyday existence, explicates it in diverse manners, and enriches it with additional symbolism, as in the case of the maze or the "cover girl" syndrome.

Robbe-Grillet's concern for thematic development of these social elements can best be seen in *Eden*, where twelve themes are cast and recast in ten series. Some of these same twelve themes will recur in his other films: blood, water, painting, male aggression linked with sperm, death, the double image, dance, labyrinth, prison, door, and light. These signs that assail him in the métro, shop windows, and magazines comprise the sociomythological world; the director refers to these gestating elements as "thèmes générateurs."[16]

Robbe-Grillet has often alluded to the fact that he is constantly preoccupied by the image of the labyrinth and chooses to scrutinize it in his literary and cinematic works. Besides designating the basic narrative structures and the sound tracks as labyrinthine expressions, he has produced elaborate and intricate variations of this primordial form within the content itself. From microcosms to macrocosms, the image is represented in diverse forms, as in the Tunisian village in *Eden* and the city of Istanbul in *L'Immortelle*. In the latter film, the physical labyrinth as well as the oriental language, customs, and psychology of the place instill in N a sensation of being an alien in this world. The inn and the château of *L'Homme* engender in Boris a similar uneasiness, as noted previously. The baroque palace and gardens of *Marienbad* depend upon one's interpretation—man's bewilderment, a mental hospital, or a bourgeois coffin. The TEE and Café Eden become palaces of illusion through the use of mirrorlike surfaces, an integral part of the thematic approach of the director. The subterranean passages of *Glissements* assume a part of the mythology directed against alleged repression by civil and religious authorities in contemporary society. The labyrinth of the stockroom in this film and that of *L'Homme* appear to be more aesthetic compositions than reflections of society, whereas shots of the métro at the Gare du Nord in *TEE* have some critical bearing upon the zombielike life-style of the commuters. In his recent films, the director chooses to blend more and more the sociological with the aesthetic.

Within the past few decades there has evolved a significant interest in play and in the ritual moments of man's life in an attempt to realize a certain balance with his serious, workday mentality. Jung, Eliade, Huizinga, and Campbell have raised our consciousness of this side of humanity. Discussing his film *Le Jeu avec le feu*, Robbe-Grillet in the spirit of Harvey Cox in *A Feast of Fools* presents his own sophisticated usage of play in his works:

> I have been diametrically opposed to the pejorative connotation which our sad-eyed culture attaches to the word "play." For my part, play is synonymous with invention, liberty, and life itself. Moreover, contemporary sociologists and psychologists have discovered the necessity to re-introduce the notion of "play" into our robot-like existence.[17]

In analyzing the use of this phenomenon in the director's films, we find that it is situated on several levels: actual games or rituals, the actor's playing out of the character, and that of Robbe-Grillet's amusing relationship with the spectator.

The game is a vital component of *Marienbad* where it takes on multiple forms, as in the ancient, sixteen-element game of Nim, dominoes, and cards. M always wins at these games, but in the end X takes possession of the prize, A. The sport of marksmanship has a rather Freudian meaning for Resnais and Robbe-Grillet in relation to sexual impotency, but this was eventually toned down in the final version of the film.

The Café Eden welcomes the bored members of university society who come together to involve themselves in numerous exotic and exciting games, such as Russian roulette, collective rape, drinking of blood, and the like. Excitation and adventure thus lift them out of their existential state of ennui, as Robbe-Grillet pinpoints some of the problems of the younger generation. Making an allusion to the biblical origin of this paradise, the director situates these games in the film:

> The games in the Garden of Eden were very innocent. Once cast out of Eden, man and woman finally realized that they still had the power to

play. Only their innocence disappeared. Throughout the film (*L'Eden*) the young girl's game of initiation is played out in her imagination.[18]

In the early stages of his film career, as is obvious from the minute instructions in his two *ciné-romans*, Robbe-Grillet required perfect correspondence of the actor's gestures and expressions to the established scenario, all worked out with geometric precision. As his experience increased, the scenario became less precise, as in the case of *TEE* and *Eden*. It was more open to spontaneity during the actual filming, with greater reliance upon the interpretation of the actors who assimilated the role and added to its fuller realization. A good illustration would be the director's experimentation in *L'Homme*, in which he asked Jean-Louis Trintignant to improvise his character Boris in one of the later sequences in the film. Spontaneously, but with difficulty, Trintignant did so, and then rewrote the dialogue and performed the new interpretation the next day. In the role of Elias in *TEE*, the same actor goes through the movements of a convincing, sadistic rape of Eva, but at the conclusion of their encounter, the couple discuss objectively how each responded and played the game. The director has his character Elias truly "play out" his passion.

With each film Robbe-Grillet entertains himself and his public with a wide range of humorous or literary allusions, as, for instance, Jean-Louis Trintignant (Elias) standing in front of a James Bond poster (*To Russia with Love*) in *TEE*, in the same stance as Belmondo stood before a Bogart poster in *Breathless*. The film viewer is faced with a gamut of amusing situations when Robbe-Grillet begins playing with mirrors, reflections, stereotypes, and comic episodes, as Elias in *TEE* lecherously reading a Japanese pornography magazine tucked in another magazine, or an actor winking to the public. With *L'Homme*, the game is truth or lie, as the director leads his audience around and around in a circle with no exit.

At certain moments in his films, the game is elevated to a sense of ritual, which has some correlation with the collective unconscious and a social mythology. In *Glissements*, Alice ceremoniously dresses and undresses Nora. Later in the film, both prostitutes perform a ritual rape on a mannequin and then carve it in blood during a very surrealistic scene on the beach. (The mannequin will reappear in his 1976 novel *Topologie d'une cité fantôme*.) Another more ambiguous ritual occurs as Alice covers the naked body of Nora with eggs and then pours a red syrup over her. All of these gestures are carried out slowly, carefully, and with almost a sacred deliberateness. In *L'Homme*, the game becomes a ritual for the three women as Maria is tried for allowing herself to be seduced by the stranger. The scene is played out almost in silence with theatrical gestures. In the script, Robbe-Grillet alludes to his attempt to create a sense of reverence in the ritual trial and execution by having communion offered to the victim Maria by the high priestess Laura.[19] A final example of this ritual preoccupation can be found in *Le Jeu*; as cited previously, Carolina opens each door in the bordello and witnesses various sexual perversions ritually acted out. In general, this heightened sense of ritual in Robbe-Grillet's works harmonizes well with his stylized decor and action, and adds to the sensual plasticity of his works.

Another fascination of the director is the double image. As with the labyrinth, its concretization is varied, appearing in unusual, but aesthetically pleasing forms and showing a reality fractured, mirrored, or duplicated. Beginning with the characterization in *Marienbad*, we see the actress in the play staged at the hotel yielding to her seducer with, "Je suis à vous," and A playing out the exact same role at the conclusion of the film. A thus incorporates the identity of this woman. The similarity between the statue and the couple in this film is also obvious. *TEE* reveals Robbe-Grillet and his wife Catherine as creators and subjects of the action. In *Eden*, after the stranger dies, he or his double appears again in Djerba. Violette and her "twin" in this film resemble a shot of the two women in Bergman's *Persona*, especially with their short blond hair and look-alike minidresses. In the Tunisian desert, the appearance of the double perhaps enters the state of mirage.

Glissements and *Le Jeu* both contain duplicate characters involved in some aspect of sexual activity. In *Glissements*, the attractive Maître David bears a striking resemblance to Alice's companion Nora and dies tied to the bed as the young sorceress's victim. *Le Jeu* becomes more controversial as the father of Carolina de Saxe also plays the role of her lover in the bordello.

Apart from this characterization, there is the duplication of scenes. *L'Immortelle* presents the accident of the French professor as an echo of that of the mysterious L. At the end of *TEE*, the director and company arrive at their destination and read in the paper that the double murder that they planned for the film had just taken place. There is a double poisoning of Boris in *L'Homme*, and the "reconstruction" of the crime in *Glissements* staged to prove the guilt of the accused Alice, results in the second murder of Maître David/Nora.

The mirror—already almost a cliché with Cocteau's *Le Sang d'un poète* in 1930—is utilized by Robbe-Grillet as another reflection of the action and characters, perhaps as part of the identity of the latter objectified and refracted. The mirror in *Marienbad*, capturing the existential faces of the clientele in the reception hall, in A's room, and then in the bar, adds another dimension to the claustrophobic ambiance. With *L'Homme* the atmosphere of duplicity is heightened by the surrounding mirrors and reflections. The ornate TEE with its glass-paneled corridors doubling the image of the voyager reiterates the theme of the labyrinth and the concept of the film within a film. Robbe-Grillet thus can create the illusion of another form of reality as well as highlight the ambivalence and duplicity of a particular situation. As with the structure, the director raises the puzzling question, "What is really real?"

Several of Robbe-Grillet's films exhibit an obsession with blood, although it is not as realistically exploited as the bloody violence of certain recent American films such as *Straw Dogs, Deliverance, Taxi Driver,* or *Bonnie and Clyde*. Robbe-Grillet's treatment of blood is more stylized and ritualistic. For example, Boris Varissa is shot and bleeds, but the blood is washed from the shirt, and he continues on as if nothing occurred. *Eden*'s games are intimately connected with blood and death. Juxtaposed with an advertisement for Cinzano, a sign in the café encourages the client to partake of the sanguineous beverage: "BUVEZ DU SANG." *Glissements*, drawn from Michelet's *La Sorcière*, manifests a similar preoccupation of the nineteenth- and twentieth-century authors. The mannequin begins to bleed during the sexual rite; Nora and the lawyer die tied to the bed in a pool of blood; Alice, intimately describing her sexual inclinations and her menstrual experiences, implores the Protestant minister to be exorcised. Her vampiric tendencies are apparent, in relation to both her French professor and Maître David. In one of the final scenes of the film, she wanders through a labyrinth of the storeroom, wringing her hands, trying to rub the imaginary blood from them in imitation of Lady Macbeth. For brilliant coloring in the film, moreover, the paints and syrups used to mark the bodies of the sorceress as well as her victims are, of course, blood red, inspired by the paintings of Yves Klein.

The esoteric and exotic are common properties of, and intrinsic to, Robbe-Grillet's films from the *ciné-romans* to *Le Jeu*. With his creative élan, he fabricates an artificial, sensual world with its own secrets and deliberate obscurity. In terms of the esoteric, the puzzlelike quality of each film lends itself to a recherché experience: *Marienbad* is a Rorschach blot; *L'Immortelle* may occur in the mind or imagination of the French professor; the lavishly designed *TEE* is an occasion for a permanent creation. The abstruseness of *L'Homme* immediately strikes the spectator as he or she attempts to unravel the bits and pieces of Boris's tale. With a film such as *Glissements*, the parody of the Inquisition mentality mixed with the various hypotheses of Alice and the confused identity of Nora and the lawyer, all make for an arcane experience. The fear of the critics of Robbe-Grillet is that his works will only be viewed by a minimum of devotees of the cinematic cult of the director, who are specially initiated and enticed by the abstruse in his films.

As has been indicated, the director's own exotic travels as an agricultural expert in Morocco, Martinique, and Guadeloupe have become embodied in his films. With Istanbul, the colorful scenes of Turkish civilization come alive. In *Eden*, the Tunisian desert and village with their richly contrasted hues provide a visual delight to the eye. *L'Homme* and certain sequences of *Eden* have been filmed in an eerie Czechoslovakia. *Marienbad* in all its splendor is a baroque labyrinth comprising three Bavarian castles and a series of gardens. At Vincennes, the dungeon and cell where the Marquis de Sade was held prisoner for seven years serve as a thematic decor for *Glissements*.

Perhaps the most problematic side of Robbe-Grillet's films is the erotic. A connoisseur of the literary works of de Sade and Bataille, the director translates similar experiences into visual terms. In his interviews, he accentuates the fact that his erotic materials emanate from the culture itself, from a society of consumers with many, but disguised, sexual preoccupations. His chief characters all possess some type of fascination with sex, usually in a perverted fashion. The manner in which he handles them, however, is unique, according to the director, who says that he treats all these erotic images in his films in terms of stereotypes from real life. The cinematic language goes further than the simple presentation of erotic scenes. Nonetheless, Robbe-Grillet opens himself to a wide array of criticism, for he presumes to demystify the myth of sexuality while enriching and establishing it with vivid scenes in all of his films, especially in *Glissements* and *Le Jeu*. His critics, in general, however, refer to his works as traditional eroticism cast into a frozen or statuary cadre.

Most of his films display some tendency toward sadomasochism, especially concretized in the characters of Elias in *TEE* and Alice in *Glissements*. Certain scenes from *Le Jeu* re-create the same inclinations. Images of naked women, chained or tortured, pervade his cinematic world. The games in Café Eden involve a collective rape. Robbe-Grillet's original intentions for *Marienbad* included a realistic rape of A, but Resnais converted this scene into something more symbolic, giving A the appearance of an exotic white bird in distress.

Robbe-Grillet's treatment of women has become rather controversial in an era when women rightly reject the image of sex object. He portrays them sometimes divinized or reigning supremely, and at other times as objects of some obsessed male, in the spirit of Buñuel's *Belle de Jour* or *Tristana*. This attitude toward women was challenged by one of the female participants in the France Culture radio program, but the filmmaker's wife came to his defense by saying that it is dangerous and impossible to distinguish between masculine and feminine phantasms. Robbe-Grillet takes a double view of woman as goddess and sex toy from the plastic ambiance around him, as, for example, in the "cover girl" mentality found in the magazine *Elle*.[20] He draws a parallel here between these images and his films, for in both, the young women are at the peak of their beauty, their faces without blemishes or wrinkles, frozen for eternity as Greek goddesses sculptured in marble. Time is thus negated. Recalling Antonioni's *Blow Up*, the photographer snaps Alice in her cell in a parody of this model mentality.

To understand Robbe-Grillet's presentation of the erotic in his films, one must examine his intentions and philosophy. He views society as laboring under a Sisyphean burden of superstitions and restrictions ranging from civil film censorship to religious traditions and principles. These prevent the natural man from being free, and it is only the sorceress à la Michelet who becomes the liberated ideal in challenging the established suffocators of society.[21] On the other hand, Robbe-Grillet feels that man himself creates these restrictions because of his fear of total emancipation. Robbe-Grillet's purpose as director, especially in a film such as *Glissements*, is to push back the barriers of hypocrisy. His critics, nonetheless, accuse him of the same hypocrisy in his selection of sexual material to please the voyeur in each individual and not simply to serve as a parody or social message.

The case of eroticism in the director's films is not clear-cut. In one sense, he enters into the commercial world of marketable sex, and in another, he says he develops this material in order to force society to reflect upon its values and norms. He refuses to be called a moralist, but with his last two films he plays on this field. He wishes to creatively raise these issues without offering structured responses. At one moment he states that his material comes from the comic book world in order to serve as a stereotyped reflection of society, but at the same time he exploits the erotic side of women, especially treating them as sadistic pleasure objects in such films as *TEE* and *Le Jeu*. The archetypes and stereotypes are all present, yet one can never be certain if Robbe-Grillet, in orchestrating them, is forcing an issue, desacralizing the mystique of sex, appealing to the "natural" and "instinctual" in man, destroying authoritarian repression, or commercializing his sexual merchandise under a disguise of satire or social critique.

As one examines the cinematic contributions of Robbe-Grillet, a freshness and inventiveness can be readily detected. New avenues for cinema and criticism alike have been opened because of the defiant spirit of Robbe-Grillet and others who have ventured to dispense themselves from following the golden rules of cinema. (Robbe-Grillet prides himself on having come into the world of literature without any "literary baggage," and then into that of film without any "cinematic baggage.") With some historical perspective, nevertheless, one can see that the surrealist film directors/artists of the early 1930s (Buñuel, Dali, Léger, Dulac, Clair, and the others) manifested the same tendencies— *écriture automatique*, the totally unexpected, a collapse of time and space, and a juxtaposition of the real and the imaginary. The acceptance of their adventure in technique was only later appreciated. Robbe-Grillet's personal evolution in film technique has steadily progressed, according to the critics, who at the same time would be the first to say that his subject matter leaves something to be desired.

In his later films the director looks more closely at society and captures some of its anguish and growing pains, especially in terms of the erotic. His films, once again, supposedly contain no "message" as such, yet the material is shaped so as to pinpoint the areas of our lives that must be re-examined. In choosing or editing these elements, he already initiates a commentary on society. His films were thus at first a confrontation of technical rules, but gradually, as these rules became more and more secondary to cinéastes (to which Marguerite Duras can testify), Robbe-Grillet began to challenge society's values. Stating that he is neither Christian nor Marxist, the director feels that absolutes are dead in our society, and that we must move from this point onward.[22]

By reason of the structure and content of his films, Robbe-Grillet forces the film viewer to participate. Those who come in direct contact with his cinematic work cannot remain intelligently neutral. The spectator who accepts the challenge of Robbe-Grillet, fulfills the director's desire of embarking upon the *création permanente*.

Resnais/Robbe-Grillet: *L'Année dernière à Marienbad*, **1961.**

Robbe-Grillet: *L'Immortelle,* **1963.**

Robbe-Grillet: *Trans-Europ-Express*, **1966.**

Robbe-Grillet: *Glissements progressifs du plaisir*, **1974.**

Robbe-Grillet: *Glissements progressifs du plaisir*, **1974.**

Robbe-Grillet: *Le Jeu avec le feu,* **1974.**

Robbe-Grillet: *Glissements progressifs du plaisir*, **1974.**

7

MARGUERITE DURAS

What I am interested in is another *type of cinema.*

—*Press Conference, Cannes (1977)*

Almost every afternoon in the cinema, Suzanne, the young heroine of *Un Barrage contre le Pacifique*, attempts to escape from the "slings and arrows of outrageous fortune" created by the ennui of life in a French Indochinese colony as well as by her mother's overzealous love of her son Joseph, a disenchanted wastrel. These regular pilgrimages to the cinema serve as her entrance into a mystical and prefabricated world of fantasy. It is still the era of the silent film. The piano begins playing and the lights fade. Suzanne placidly discovers an oasis of happiness, artificially created on the screen. The image before her soothes, caresses, distracts, and consoles her soul that was scarred at an early age by misery. The power of the cinema becomes overwhelming. As a beautiful goddess of a woman passionately kisses her beau on the screen, Suzanne senses an overpowering communion of the spectators in the theater with the actors. She wishes she were in the shoes of these stars.[1]

In this passage from an early novel adapted later for the screen, the young Marguerite Duras in Indochina may be substituted for the heroine; there is no doubting the impact of the visual image on the screen for both. The episode recounted is certainly romantic. In fact, the films of Duras all deal with love, but a love absorbed by political, psychological, and societal problems. From the romanticism of her past has emerged a series of films of adult confrontations with the human condition.

As a child growing up near Saigon at a time when Malraux was struggling for social justice in his anticolonialist battle, Marguerite Duras was exposed to films of love as well as the classics. With her brother she would often see feature films as well as shorts in the local theater. One of the first films she recalls viewing was *Monsieur Beaucaire* (1924) with Rudolph Valentino. *Blue Angel* (1930) of Josef von Sternberg would also leave a lasting impression on her. Her favorite films, nevertheless, would be a Judy Garland musical and *The Wizard of Oz*.

A novelist and playwright, who was transformed into a filmmaker a decade ago, Marguerite Duras is difficult to classify in any one category of cinema. She shares the rubric of intellectual cinema with Alain Resnais and Alain Robbe-Grillet, tending more toward the literary than the strictly cinematic. Duras moves among the avant-garde of the femininist filmmakers[2] with Agnès Varda, Nelly Kaplan, Jeanne Moreau, and Nadine Trintignant, when she manifests her concern for the rights of women, as Xavière Gauthier points out in *Les Parleuses*.[3] She also dabbles in the political film of *engagement*, the realm of Costa-Gavras and Yves Boisset, especially in such films as *Jaune le soleil* and *Le Camion*. As an actively involved writer, Duras served for seven years as secretary of a Communist party cell, formed part of a writers-students committee during the May 1968 events in Paris, and affixed her name to a myriad of manifestoes in the late 1960s and early 1970s. Considering these diverse penchants of an artist such as Duras, it is best not to pigeonhole her creative genius to fit a certain mold. Instead, it is more advantageous to show how her political and literary tendencies unfold throughout her career and then to indicate the thematic pillars upon which her films are constructed.

The eye of the cinema public first alighted upon Duras when René Clément decided to make use of her novel *Un Barrage contre le Pacifique* for the film *This Angry Age* (1957) with Tony Perkins and Silvana Mangano. Although Clément's film would not come up to par with his *Jeux interdits, La Bataille du rail,* or *Monsieur Ripois*, it still managed to capture the contrasting poetic and realistic poles of Duras's text. The screenwriter Irwin Shaw facilitated the transposition to the screen of the Indochina narrative about a mother's combat with nature and her emotional involvement with her two grown children.

This Angry Age was one of the few adaptations that Duras permitted. In 1967, Jules Dassin (*Never on Sunday, Phaedra, Topkapi*) directed *10:30 P.M. Summer* based on her novel *10h30 du soir en été* published in 1960. Like *This Angry Age*, the film is commercial and star-studded—Melina Mercouri, Peter Finch, and Romy Schneider. *10:30 P.M. Summer* was but a naive rendering of the tacit complicity of Maria with the murderer Rodrigo Paesta in a small Spanish city. With its source of *Le Marin du Gibraltar* (1952) as sketched by Duras, *The Sailor from Gibraltar* of Tony Richardson (*A Taste of Honey, Tom Jones, The Loneliness of a Long Distance Runner*) of the same vintage year as *10:30 P.M. Summer* would be just as poorly received. The material in essence was there—the heartrending search for a lost love aboard the yacht *Gibraltar*—but it did not imaginatively emerge in the translation to the screen. The absence of rhythm and the lack of dramatic movement ranked this with the other previous adaptations from Duras's repertoire, proving that literal translations, or even very flowing ones with large casts and budgets, cannot succeed without absolute sensitivity to the mood of the text.

Duras was catapulted abruptly into the cinema world in 1958. Alain Resnais, well respected for his short documentaries on the concentration camps (*Nuit et brouillard*) and the Bibliothèque Nationale in Paris (*Toute la mémoire du monde*), was planning a feature film and searching for a screenwriter who could collaborate with him on the scenario. Through an intermediary, Olga Wormser, Resnais contacted Duras and invited her to furnish him with the basis for a film. The filmmaker had been acquainted with her literary work since his reading of *Le Square*. Resnais provided Duras with an algebraic conception of the film he had in mind, requesting her to write the story of the characters as if they were going to film them integrally and chronologically. As the *point de départ* of the scenario he thus requested of the novelist a biography of each individual, even though it would not be used. Resnais suggested that Duras create something in the tone of a recitative that would approach the opera in essence.[4] Resnais left her with specific instructions to take care of the literary part of the collaboration, not to be concerned with what he would do with it, and above all, to completely forget the camera.[5] They both did their part and the film *Hiroshima, mon amour*—depicting the horror of the bombing and the souvenirs of the Japanese-French couple—brought much deserved attention to Resnais and Duras starting with the Cannes Film Festival of 1959. Not all the attention would be favorable, however, for the censors in Montreal examined the work and amputated fourteen minutes from the corpus of the film, resulting in hostile picketing against censorship standards.

To the English director Peter Brook (*Lord of the Flies, Marat/Sade*), Duras and Gérard Jarlot confided *Moderato Cantabile* in 1960—the title originating from a sonata of Diabelli—but with disparaging results.[6] The film describes a wealthy woman from the provinces who relives the passionate crime of a pair of lovers before her husband rediscovers her. Spectator and critic alike found the nebulous world situated halfway between the imaginary and the real very unsettling. Despite the strong personalities of Belmondo and Moreau, *Moderato Cantabile* was considered one of the greatest disappointments of the Cannes Festival of 1960.

Henri Colpi, who edited *Nuit et brouillard, Hiroshima,* and *Marienbad* for Resnais, launched out on his own with *Une aussi longue absence*, his first feature film. Once again, Duras would pen the script and bring the film to an international audience at Cannes. She and Jarlot collaborated on a theme appreciated by Resnais, that of memories. Thérèse Langlois tries to find her lost husband in the vagabond Robert Landais. The film won the first prize at Cannes in 1961 and was also awarded the Prix Louis Delluc for the same year.

Her fourth screenplay was written for another debutant filmmaker as she had also done for Resnais and Colpi. For Jean Chapot, Duras developed the scenario of *La Voleuse* (1966), which portrays a mother who abandons her child at birth and six years later wishes to take it away from the parents who raised it.

Rarely seen would be the two short films for which Duras's work served as a basis. Karmitz in 1964 filmed *Nuit noire, Calcutta,* and Franju, well considered for his *Thérèse Desqueyroux*, completed *Les Rideaux blancs* in 1965.

At the time of her scriptwriting Duras would often repeat that she was a novelist and nothing more. Later she again would say that she was a novelist who makes films and avoided saying that she was a film director.[7] The year 1966 would be a turning point in her career. Commenting on this shift of focus as she took up the camera, Duras mentioned that she felt that she could at least do what Dassin and Richardson did with her literary work.[8] Her primary intention, however, was to have Dassin adapt her play *La Musica.* He offered to produce it instead and have his daughter Julie play a role. Duras decided to undertake the filming herself and turned to Paul Séban for technical assistance. Séban had made short films for television and had worked as an assistant to Jean Renoir, Claude Chabrol, and Joris Ivens. A middle-aged couple meet in a hotel in Evreux following their divorce, ready to begin another phase of their lives. Anne (Delphine Seyrig), perhaps a later model of Suzanne in *Un Barrage contre le Pacifique*, fell into the habit of frequenting the cinema when her relationship with Michel (Robert Hossein) grew stagnant. Now they only have memories upon which to rely.[9]

From another play, *Détruire, dit-elle*, written in the wake of the 1968 events in Paris, Duras filmed a powerful psychodrama about four people in what could be either a rest home or a resort. Evoking souvenirs of *Persona*, the two women absorb a part of each other's character as they await the arrival of Elisbeth's husband. Initially the French producers agreed to use the literary work of Duras but refused to allow her to do the filming. Obstinate, she eventually assumed full direction of the work.[10] With both her literary and cinematic undertakings she destroyed the sacrosanct classical traditions of language, characterization, chronology, and unity, just as her peers of the Nouveau Roman (Alain Robbe-Grillet and Michel Butor) did in the late 1950s and early 1960s. Her later works of *Nathalie Granger, India Song,* and *Le Camion,* which were equally as radical in technique would also share the glory of the New York Film Festival.

In filming *Détruire, dit-elle*, Duras followed the same principles that are evident in all of her works. These principles make up what she refers to as "un autre cinéma." The patterns that we can detect today are the minimal budget, with funds usually from the Centre National du Cinéma; the same crew, with Bruno Nuytten most often behind the camera; a core of actors like Michel Lonsdale, Delphine Seyrig, and Gérard Depardieu; and quick writing of a scenario and equally as rapid filming, completing *Détruire* in several days. Her principal aesthetic theory is to strip the work to its basic elements, which sometimes, however, results in a poverty of cinema or literature, according to many critics. One could not have a better illustration of this phenomenon than the filming of *Le Camion*, which was completed within a week, script in hand, and without a rehearsal. Nevertheless, throughout her films Duras proves to be the catalyst or the organizing link in the whole process, supervising and suggesting, but allowing the liberty and spontaneity of the actors to enter into the work.

In 1970, the author and now somewhat established cinéaste began planning her next film. Manifesting her uneasiness with Communist party politics, Duras wrote *Abahn Sabana David*, which may fall into the category of the Costa-Gavras/London work, *L'Aveu* (The Confession). David, accompanied by Sabana, is sent by the almighty Gringo to eliminate a Jewish worker who appears to interfere with the plans of the big boss. After a lengthy conversation with the Jewish men, David and Sabana side with the latter, recalling the May 1968 slogan—"We are all German Jews!' In filming this political narrative in 1971, Duras had originally tried to underline the racist elements in the encounter by the title *L'Ecriture bleue* with allusions to the gas chambers. She finally decided upon the title *Jaune le soleil.*

Duras structured the plot of the following film around the mother of Nathalie Granger, Isabelle, who would be played by Jeanne Moreau. When the Italian actress Lucia Bose accepted to make the film with the cinéaste, Duras shuffled the characters in the work and had Lucia assume the role of Isabelle and Jeanne her taciturn friend.[11] Filmed at Duras's country home in Neuphle-le-Château from 2 to 16 April 1972, *Nathalie Granger* could easily be called "A Day in the Life of Isabelle Granger" or

"The Diary of a Concerned Housewife." The film recounts Isabelle's difficulties with her daughter Nathalie who has violent tendencies, a visit from a frustrated salesman, and the banal, daily chores of ironing, clearing the table, and the like. *Nathalie Granger* penetrates the physical and metaphysical world of women in a slow-paced, meditative rhythm. Duras describes the film as a uterus with a pair of twins floating within and then being born,[12] a very strong parallel to the situation in the cinéaste's more recent *Baxter, Vera Baxter.*

The pace of Duras's cinematic fecundity and interest is now quickened. She finished editing *Nathalie Granger* in July 1972, wrote *La Femme du Gange* in September, and filmed it in November of the same year. With the latter film made at Trouville-sur-mer, Duras entered another world. Side by side with *India Song* and *Son nom de Venise dans Calcutta désert*, this film helps to comprise what might be considered as Duras's "Indian trilogy." Unlike Satyajit Ray's trilogy—*The World of Apu, Aparajito,* and *Pather Panchali*—Duras's work deals with *another* India. During a group discussion around Duras following the release of *India Song*, an Indian woman said that the film did not portray the real India. The filmmaker, who visited Calcutta for only two hours at the age of seventeen, was quick to point out that her intention was to create the country visualized in her mind and not an India of a documentary film. The places and distances were deliberately falsified. Furthermore, there was no possibility of filming on location; instead it would be an "Inde métaphorique."[13] The India of *La Femme du Gange* would be that of the French ambassador's wife, Anne-Marie Stretter, as filtered through the mind of the traveler in the seaside town of S. Thala. Before the choice of this title, other possibilities flowed through Duras's mind: *Les Amants du Gange, Les Iles, Le Ciel de mousson, La Route de Delta,* and *La Route de Chandernago.*

La Femme du Gange logically led to her next film. *India Song,* originally requested by Peter Hall of the National Theatre in London in 1972, emerged as a more elaborate cinematic venture both technically and psychologically. It would flesh out the principal characters from Duras's novel *Le Vice-Consul.* Through the melodic voices of the young women in the background of the film, the narrative of the characters in an imaginary Calcutta of the 1930s—like the ambiance of *Marienbad* in the same epoch—is leisurely pieced together. Anne-Marie Stretter (Delphine Seyrig) is followed to the embassy in Calcutta by the blindly amorous Michael Richardson (Claude Mann). He is only one among many, for the charms of the bored Anne-Marie Stretter are distributed widely. In the course of a reception at the embassy, while Anne-Marie Stretter is surrounded by members of the diplomatic corps, the vice-consul (Michel

Lonsdale), in a state of frenzy, begins to howl, filling the nocturnal streets of Calcutta with Anne-Marie's maiden name—Anna Maria Guardi. The ambassador's wife later meets her death on the islands and is buried in the English cemetery. The film, appreciated at Cannes as a very sensitive, albeit recherché, study of these disembodied creatures, was less enthusiastically received by Vincent Canby of the *New York Times* who paints it as a "four-hankie story," dealing with leprosy of the body as well as the soul.[14]

The producers Pierre and François Barat, who thrive on taking risks, asked Duras to film a sequel to *India Song*. She was very reluctant and yet felt that her obsession with India had not subsided. Utilizing the sound track of *India Song* and reconstructing the château of Paris's sixteenth arrondissement into the dilapidated embassy haunted by its previous occupants, she embarked upon a daring venture—*Son nom de Venise dans Calcutta désert*. The weariness of embassy life comes across vividly in the decor and the voices that are deliberately not synchronized with the image.

Des Journées entières dans les arbres—a novel in 1953, a play in 1965, evolved into a film in 1977. The basic experiences of the author from the mother-son relationship she witnessed as a child in her family have crystallized in different aesthetic forms. In late 1976, Madeleine Renaud in an astounding manner, incarnated for the stage (Théâtre d' Orsay of Renaud/Barrault) the rich, almost senile mother who returns to Paris from a former French colony to visit her wayward son Jacques (Jean-Pierre Aumont). He is presently living with Marcelle (Bulle Ogier), a sympathetic nightclub hostess/dancer, and blindly gambling away his life as well as his relationships. For the cinematic adaptation Duras altered some of the dialogue. The crew filmed during the day and staged the play at night with occasional confusion at times in the modified lines. With *Des Journées*, in a sense, we return to the realm of the *théâtre filmé* of Guitry and Pagnol, for the camera moves very little, whereas the action is limited to what could basically be a two-set stage—the apartment and the bar. The silences, which occupy such a privileged place in Duras's cinematic repertoire, punctuate the crisp dialogues, interspersed with the incoherent mumblings of the mother who is madly concerned about her son's welfare as he wastes away his life far from her bosom.

While *Des Journées* was attracting a large theater public, Duras was already planning her next work—*Baxter, Vera Baxter*, subtitled *Les Plages de l'Atlantique*. The work evokes the atmosphere of close to a thousand years ago, when the men were away on the crusades and the solitary women began to speak with the trees, animals, or sea, and were immediately burned as sorceresses. Duras's usual crew of actors was on hand, including Gérard Depardieu and Delphine Seyrig, but with Sacha Vierny behind the camera instead of Bruno Nuytten.

Vera Baxter (Claudine Gabay), the thirty-eight-year-old wife of a businessman whose career oscillates between wealth and ruin, is a dedicated spouse and mother to three children. She receives a visit from an unknown woman (Delphine Seyrig), and the time the two women spend together in a type of enclosed aquarium allows for a revelation of Vera's relationship with her unfaithful husband Jean. The final blow comes when Vera learns that her husband paid a man to commit adultery with her. The tragic and fragile relationship of Jean and Vera was and always will be based on money.

Baxter, Vera Baxter was screened at Cannes in 1977 in the *Marché du Film* series, whereas *Le Camion* of the same vintage year was presented in the official competition with two other French films, *Un Taxi mauve* (Boisset) and *La Communion solennelle* (Feret). Duras's *Le Camion* reflects her threefold talent—screenwriter, director, and actress. Her script can be considered a political monologue delivered by an enigmatic middle-aged woman to the truck driver, a Communist and union worker, who offers her a lift. The film touches upon areas that gravely affect our society—racism, the problems of the proletariat, the inefficacy of communism, cosmic fear, and the like. The result is a type of film within a film in which lyrical scenes of the blue truck are interspersed with a reading of the script by Gérard Depardieu and Marguerite Duras. *Le Camion*, dividing the critics because of its radical nature, reflects a fragment of the quasi-nihilistic theory of Duras that the world and the cinema can go to rack and ruin.[15]

At the press conference at Cannes in 1977, Duras was asked if she would continue in literature, given her almost full-time dedication to cinema (with her contribution of ten films). She hesitated and then said she could not offer a response for the moment. For her next film project, however, she intended to adapt her novel *Les Petits Chevaux de Tarquina* (1953) with Maria Schneider as one of the principal characters, but other projects intervened.

In late July and early August 1978, Duras re-created quickly and *ex nihilo* a universe of solitude and despair around a trio of characters, enigmatically played by Dominique Sanda, Bulle Ogier, and Mathieu Carrière. In *Le Navire 'Night,'* finely composed shots of river banks, cemetery, and intersections create a contrapuntal experience with the haunting melodies of the voices, aesthetically pleasing both eye and ear. Once again we are far from the rational furrows of traditional cinema.

All of a sudden the cinéaste changes film genres, from the almost-two-hour-long, quasi-commercial production of *Le Camion* to a unique series of short films. This radical shift would be equivalent to a novelist's turning to short stories or perhaps even sonnets for self-expression. In the fall of 1979, Duras released four such cameos: *Césarée* (color, 11 min.), *Les Mains négatives* (color, 16 min.), *Aurélia Steiner* (color, 30 min.), and *Auréla Steiner* (black-and-white, 45 min.). Usually with Amy Flammer providing the cello background to the film and Pierre Lhomme the images, Duras would weave an eerie and hermetic tale in a voice-off that would not correspond to the image on the screen but would aurally enrich the exotic visual experience.

In the cinematic universe of Marguerite Duras, besides her sensitivity to the image that carries over from her literary expression, her reliable crew of actors and technicians, and the deliberate disregard for classical cinema rules, there are several other pervading constants. These are recurrent personages, leitmotifs, and elements, some of which have been recorded by Alain Vircondelet in 1972,[16] before the "Indian trilogy" and her most recent films from 1976 to 1979. Vircondelet analytically deciphers the thematic treatment of love, death, destruction, and madness, mostly in speaking of her literary world. Duras's films reveal some of the same preoccupations but go one step further since these leitmotifs are concretized and reinforced by sounds and images. Let us examine some of the intricate components of her more recently created universe.

When he was interviewed during the filming of *India Song* in 1975, the actor Claude Juan referred to the cinematic domain of Duras as "un monde clos."[17] For her characters surrounded by the walls of an embassy or a home, or a forest, there is no exit. The atmosphere is hermetic and ambiguity reigns supreme. For the characters in *Détruire* the subtle shifts of identify may lose some of the spectators, whereas the "voices off" in a film such as *Son nom de Venise dans Calcutta désert* provide the only link to what has happened in the past at the French Embassy of Calcutta. One critic caustically remarked in passing that all Duras does in her films is to situate her camera in a certain position and let it film the lack of action taking place. Nevertheless, it is atmosphere and not action that the filmmaker seeks to create, an atmosphere that is usually marked by the lassitude that is so common to our contemporary society. Like a gray foreboding cloud, it hovers over the hotels of *La Femme du Gange* or *10:30 P.M. Summer*, the French Embassy of *India Song* or *Son nom de Venise*, and the convalescent home/resort of *Détruire*. In *Nathalie Granger*, after the two women finish the dishes, they sense the hollow (*creux*) of the afternoon; it weighs heavily upon them. There is a world-weariness that prevails in this ambiance, which suffocates the characters psychologically. They are rarely involved in any type of actual physical work, with the exception of Isabelle Granger as housewife, or the Communist truck driver of *Le Camion*. As a result, the characters appear to move about in slow motion, like zombies, eyes directly ahead, hands often rigidly at their side—a reentry into the zone of *Marienbad*.

The weather ordinarily underscores the state of soul, and hence reinforces this ennui in Duras's films. The balmy climate of *Un Barrage* as well as that of *Son nom de Venise* stifles the psyche and the gestures of the characters. They can barely move, suffocating in the heat, and fall prey to the forces of their social milieu. Vircondelet depicts these individuals as victims of a cocoon that they themselves have spun.[18]

The contrast of decadence with misery forms an integral part of the social as well as political universe of the filmmaker. The wealthy suitors of Suzanne in *Un Barrage* (This Angry Age), unconcerned about their careless expenditure of money in the Indochinese colony, are diametrically opposed to the mother (Mme Dufresne in the Clément film) who scrapes and scrimps for every cent in order to keep the rice paddies in operation. Duras's political awareness was certainly sparked as a young girl witnessing the children in the colony dying from malnutrition and being buried in their own yards, or else peasants in agony whittling away to nothing by unknown illnesses. At the same time the rich colonialists continued to exploit the lower classes, employing them in their grandiose money-making projects.

The divergence of social levels in *India Song* is especially obvious. Around the embassy where little happens outside of the receptions, a strange aroma wafts gently through the air—the crematoria of Calcutta, in full operation, burning the bodies of the natives dying of leprosy or malnutrition. During a reception the voice of an Indian woman beggar reaches the ears of the members of the diplomatic corps. She is the eternal mendicant whose pleas cry out to the heavens for justice in this world. Alongside her are the lepers—those in the streets and alleyways of Calcutta who experience a leprosy of the body, and those in the French Embassy who suffer from the leprosy of the soul. It is uncertain who is more to be pitied.

In *Des Journées* which could serve as a sequel to the final section of *Un Barrage contre le Pacifique* where the restless Joseph heads off to the city, Jacques squanders his (and his mother's) money gambling. Made in the same image as Jean Baxter, he remains a child, never accepting responsibility or a stable situation with the people in his life. The unsympathetic character makes a victim of his mother and Marcelle. His relationship with his companion is ephemeral.

Further tension infiltrates the realm of Duras—the powerful, destructive rulers of society versus their prey who must metaphorically creep on all fours at their feet. The landowners of *Un Barrage* oppose their underlings who every day struggle to find sufficient nourishment. In the novel the mother of Joseph and Suzanne writes a powerful letter to the smug government officials describing in detail their victims. One does not expect that the letter will be heeded.[19]

In speaking of *Détruire*, Duras denounces all power—religious, police, intellectual, and Communist.[20] *Jaune le soleil* reflects the cinéaste's disenchantment with the leaders of a political movement who direct the lives of the simple adherents to the party, like David, obliged to take every wish of the domineering chiefs as a command. Duras refers to this type of politicized subservience as "automutilation," self-destruction in its most abject dehumanizing form. In *Le Camion*, the anti-Communist sentiment is still present. The middle-aged woman of the film voices Duras's reflections about the inequalities of society, mostly racist, which find their parallel in *Jaune le soleil* (anti-Semitic) and *Nathalie Granger* (anti-Portuguese).

Though no one is actually seen dying in her films, death is always in the wings, hovering like a voracious vulture waiting for its next cadaver. The rice paddies and the streets of Calcutta reek of the dead, and the smell of burned flesh never leaves Hiroshima. As a means of recording the passage of time in *Nathalie Granger* the filmmaker utilizes a radio news report of youths who killed three people without mercy or reason. Anne-Marie Stretter lies dead in the English cemetery in India, and Elisabeth of *Détruire* requires convalescence following a miscarriage. A crime of passion in the café of *Moderato Cantabile* leaves a dead victim whose story Anne compulsively desires to learn. What is at times worse than this type of death, is the death-warmed-over attitude that the characters assume, not unlike that of the old Doctor Isaac Borg in *Wild Strawberries*. Their gestures, emotions, and glances reflect little remaining life in the languishing souls of these individuals. Voices are estranged from their bodies, as in the Indian trilogy.

At times the only life that beats through the veins of the characters is musical. Throughout Duras's novels and films music fills the weary or boring interludes of human existence. From *Un Barrage* to *India Song*[21] a delicate melody lightens the atmosphere: "Ramona" of *Un Barrage*, "Blue Moon" of *La Femme du Gange*, and "India Song" in the other two Indian films. The seven notes of the piano hesitatingly played by Nathalie Granger in the film create a simple but meaningful background, given music's calming power for the child, and as a musical motif throughout the film it renders her present even when she is out of the house. Part of the link with the past for Thérèse Langlois in *Une aussi longue absence* is the vagabond's singing of a tune from Rossini's *Barber of Seville*. What could be more soul-stirring than the elderly mother of *Des Journées* waltzing the "Blue Danube" with her son at the nightclub? Bach's Fugue No. 15 from the *Art of the Fugue* serves as a background for *Détruire*, *dit-elle*, and Diabelli's compositions inspire the musical accompaniments for *Moderato Cantabile* (a sonata) and *Son nom de Venise* (Beethoven's fourteenth variation on a theme from Diabelli). In *Le Camion*, Diabelli's music follows the lyrical passage of the truck. Amy Flammer's cello arrangements for the short films of 1979 create a cosmic aura with the rich images.

For Duras, music has become an integral part of every level of the film. Jack Gousseland described how the author of *La Musica* wrote as if for an opera, with certain musical phrasing, repetitions, and cadence.[22] *Hiroshima* was planned like a recitative. The music, furthermore, will be absolutely essential to create the *état d'âme*, or the psychological mood of the characters. The gradually descending triplets of *India Song* composed by Carlos d'Allesio capture the lassitude of the 1930s. The same composer is also responsible for the original music constructed around the rhumba in *Baxter, Vera Baxter*. Like the haunting voices of *Marienbad*, the voices of the characters—sometimes offstage as in *India Song*—also create a type of polyphony that has been referred to as "mélopée lyrique" by Vircondelet.[23] This often results from the play of accents in the work, discovered perhaps by Duras with Resnais in *Hiroshima*.

The music often heard in a dance hall or at a reception supposedly offers an escape from the monotony of daily life. The robots appear to be dancing on automatic pilot. In the dance halls of the 1920s and 1930s, nonetheless, the Durassian inhabitants are as bored with their dance as with the rest of their existence.

At the same time that music predominates, silence aesthetically fills in the remainder of the film. Dialogues are few and the blanks are very important. Jean-Louis Barrault and Duras in speaking of her work observed that blanks and silences often count more than words. A metaphysical silence hovers over the set of *Des Journées* as Madeleine Renaud just sits and stares after her arrival in Paris, or as she ravenously devours the meal set before her. Only her incoherent mutterings disturb the calm.

Duras's dramatic work and her films depend heavily upon the mood of silence. Vircondelet, for example, counted sixty-five moments of silence in the text of *Détruire*, and her other theater and cinema works reflect this same penchant. *Baxter, Vera Baxter*'s glacial ambiance is partly a result of the minimal exchange between Vera and the visitor, punctuated by hesitations and silences. An occasional "perhaps" or "I don't think" emerge from some very deep interior source of their beings, whereas the simplest words are pronounced in a sententious tone, heavy with reflection.

Often enough the silence is found in conjunction with waiting, made popular in contemporary theater by Beckett's *En attendant Godot* and refracted through the ennui that directionless people feel. In many ways the silence does not indicate a period of reflection but a refusal to speak or a sense of a vacuum. The emptiness weighs heavily upon these characters, and they become fossilized. Their communication breaks down, as in the case of the traveling salesman entering the silent domain of the women in *Nathalie Granger*. He has his words conveniently packaged to sell his product. Isabelle and her friend, on the other hand, are at ease in being silent, a comfortableness that we also observe in the many pauses of *Baxter, Vera Baxter.*

During the press conference at Cannes following the showing of *Le Camion*, Duras, playing on words, said that this work is "un film sur tout." She said it dealt with everything, but primarily with love, a general sense of love. Love and madness dovetail perfectly in this unknown middle-aged hitchhiker. Perhaps she is an escapee from a local mental hospital, suggests Depardieu in reading the script with Duras. The juxtaposition of love and madness in her universe produces an enigmatic environment. Unrequited love leads to certain phases of folly, creating the anguish that is characteristic of all of her work. Let us try to separate the two elements if possible.

In *This Angry Age* the mother's distorted love for the son throughout his escapades devours her right to the very end. She feels that others might think she is mad, but the elderly woman is obsessed with keeping her enterprise going and lavishly heaping her love and concern upon an unresponsive son. The brother-sister relationship of Suzanne and Joseph recalls the delirious love shared by "les enfant terribles" of Cocteau, and more recently by the duo in *Les Enfants du placard* of Benoît Jacquot.

Moderato Cantabile reveals a wealthy Anne scarred by marital failure, struggling to discover more about the crime of passion. She desperately tries to develop a liaison with Chauvin, a former employee of her husband. When the latter comes to look for her in the café, Anne lets out the same scream as the murdered woman. The twenty-year-old "Elle" of *Hiroshima* has a strange air about her as her love for the German soldier is thwarted. Head shaved, eyes deeply set within their sockets, she hovers on the threshold of madness, incarcerated in the dark cellar. At a later stage, the love shared by the Japanese architect and the French actress is frustrated, perhaps doomed to failure, just as the earlier French-German liaison during the war. Love, ideally, has no limits, but a culture, war, and painful memories certainly are mitigating factors. Rupture and destruction often conclude many relationships in Duras's works, as in the divorced couple of *La Musica*, Alan and Sheila's relationship in *The Sailor from Gibraltar*, or the lethal action of Jean toward his faithful wife in *Baxter, Vera Baxter*.

Michael Richardson's unconditioned and obstinate love for Anne-Marie Stretter leads him to abandon his fiancée and journey to the ends of the earth in pursuit of her charms. From the S. Thala of *La Femme du*

Gange to the Calcutta of *India Song* he longs for her love, so negligently diffused among her court of admirers. The vice-consul, also obsessed with the ambassador's wife, remarks that he will make a scene if she does not respond to his love. Rejected, he screams her name throughout the streets of Calcutta, frightening the beggers as well as the cats.

Love is refracted through the characters of *Détruire* in a multitude of ways. Elisabeth feels estranged from her husband Bernard after an affair with a young doctor. Convalescing, she constantly takes sleeping pills to forget her pains of love and sorrow. Elisabeth is attracted by the young Alissa Thor, wife of Max, who is the cultic object of Stein. Their futures are open to any number of possibilities, but one senses that the tragic will predominate.

Jacques's mother returns to Paris in *Des Journées* to make a final effort to rekindle some form of filial love in his heart. The almost senile woman passively allows herself to be exploited by him in the lounge with expensive champagne, as well as in the apartment when he steals her jewels to exchange for funds for his gambling adventures. His relationship with Marcelle is also tenuous and may soon end on a disheartening note.

Vera Baxter's fidelity to the *concept* of fidelity is remarkable, especially when we learn that everything in the life of the married couple has its basis in money. Their marriage has proved to be a one-way street.

Failure thus ordinarily seems to mark the love relationship of the filmmaker's characters. They are condemned never to be fully happy with their lives and loves, and are abandoned to their private hells. The mysterious hitchhiker of *Le Camion* may offer an exception. Despite her tears and her sudden rupture of any rapport with the truck driver, she may be happy, for she refuses to search for meaning in her life.

On the other side of the coin lies madness. Duras once remarked very philosophically in an interview that she is pleased in a sense that the mental hospitals are full.[24] This indicates that our present society is insupportable, unbearable for normal, human existence. She intimates, therefore, that changes are absolutely necessary. Duras lauds the liberated sentiments of the mad, opposing these emancipated individuals to the bourgeois, imprisoned by their wealth, social standing, and so on. The mentally disturbed exhibit childlike innocence and often lack the harsh memories that destroy our lives, as exemplified in "le fou" of *La Femme du Gange*. The woman begger and the vice-consul of *India Song* are also victims of mania, in one case inflicted by society, in the other by Anne-Marie Stretter.

The cinematic and literary works of Duras have been drawn in one way or another from her own biography, and certain patterns can thus be detected. One of the contrasts that immediately strikes the view or reader of Marguerite Duras's opus is the maternity/paternity model. Xavière

Gauthier and Duras commented upon the absence of the father of Nathalie Granger in the film. His departure for his job leaves the home tranquilly occupied by the two women, symbolic, in the mind of Gauthier, of the usual hostility of male presence. Duras told her interviewer that she never really had a father, a factor that is obvious in many of the author's novels and plays.[25] The novel of *Un Barrage*, perhaps more so than the screen adaptation, reveals the explicit nonpresence of a father, with concomitant results in the upbringing of the children. Jacques of *Des Journées* is an older model of the son Joseph, grown up without a father, irresponsible, loose-living, without roots. The businessman of *Moderato Cantabile* has little time for his wife and eight-year-old son. We never see Jean Baxter, and his family rarely shares his company. He communicates with them often through letters and telegrams containing either money or lies. The husband of the hitchhiker in *Le Camion* is completely eliminated from the script. Negative paternal images abound.

One of the most haunting autobiographical elements in Duras's films and literary pieces deals with her mother, Marie Legrand. When the novelist had just published *Des Journées entières dans les arbres* (1953), she went to visit her mother who had a house in the Loire Valley. The elderly woman, dressed in a funereal black dress, refused to embrace her daughter or even to speak to her. Then the mother told her that she did not know why Marguerite invented such a story about a mother's love for her son, and that she had been certain of raising the children without favorites. Duras tried to explain to her mother that at times the love shown for a favorite is unconsciously manifest in an infinite variety of ways and perceived very sensitively by the other children. Duras left her saddened mother on her bed, after being told how much better she would have done to have gone into business instead of writing as a profession. Duras's mother died at the age of eighty, only wanting to see her eldest son. As the son and mother embraced for the last time, crying, says Duras stung by the rejection, they did not even see her.[26]

Following *Un Barrage* the mother-son relationship, fraught with love and anguish, would recur in *Moderato Cantabile* and *Des Journées entières dans les arbres*.[27] The mother will go to any extreme to please the son who, at the same time, fails to respond to the maternal concern. The filmmaker speaks of a mad love that encompasses all. The mother/martyr of *Un Barrage*, with a basis in Duras's life, struggles to create some semblance of an existence for her children out of the shambles of a miserable condition of poverty in Indochina. The mother's daily obsession with food and money would filter through the works of Duras and stay with her today, she would say.

Duras, as early as 1959, admits being haunted by the motif of memory and forgetfulness, which was precious to Resnais as is manifest in

Marienbad and *Hiroshima*.[28] The latter evokes harsh souvenirs of a frustrated love during the war. The searching traveler of *La Femme,* returning to the hotel, dance hall, and beach of S. Thala, hopes to recover his lost memories of a past love. Thérèse Langlois in *Une aussi longue absence* fashions the vagabond collecting old newspapers into the image of her absent husband.

Ingmar Berman's remark that all filming is a return to one's childhood was realized in making *Wild Strawberries*, his trilogy, and *Cries and Whispers*. Duras's film career is also a return to the fountain of her youth—economic problems in Indochina, family relationships especially with her mother and two brothers and the absence of a father, and impressions of Calcutta at the age of seventeen or eighteen. Some of these elements helped in her political evolution that would serve as another level of her creation. Her works, *grosso modo*, represent variations on a theme of love and madness, death and destruction, maternity and paternity. With her growing repertoire she taps the sentiments of the modern cinema (albeit in a recherché manner) that Gilles Jacob signals—solitude, alienation, presence of death, confrontation with time, multiple interpretations possible in each work, and the depersonalization process of the individual.[29] Her films referred to as intellectual and iconoclastic indicate another stage in the personal creative process of the novelist, playwright, and filmmaker. Writing a book, Duras feels, is a closed experience. When she films a work, however, she opens the literary piece in a new and refreshing way to the public, and demands them to actively participate in the destruction/reconstruction process—in aesthetics as well as the socio-economic phases of contemporary society. To witness is already to begin participating.

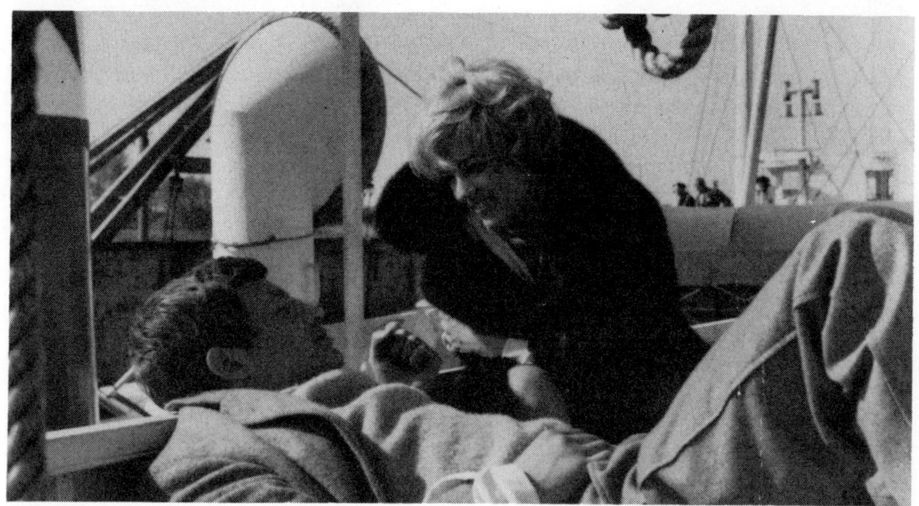

Peter Brook/Duras: *Moderato Cantabile*, **1960.**

Duras: *Nathalie Granger*, **1972.**

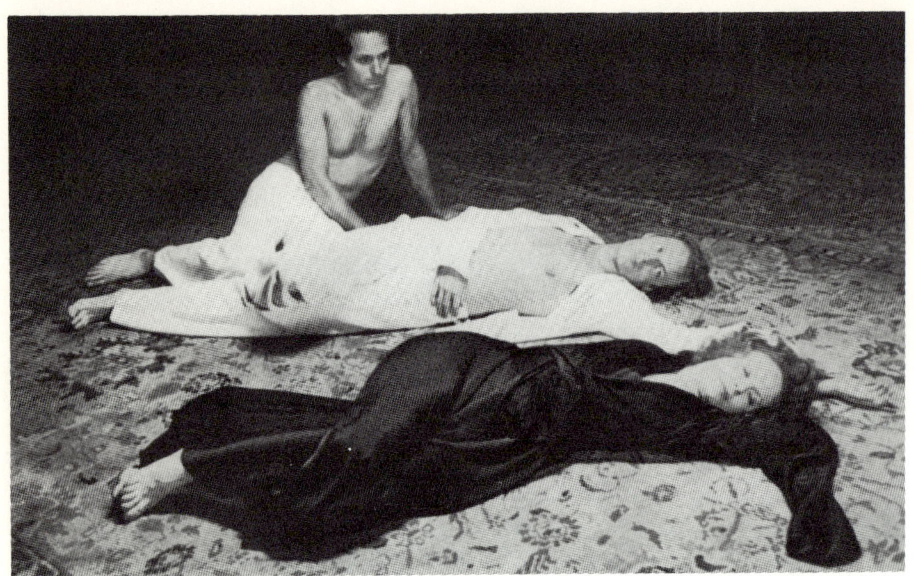

Duras: *India Song*, **1975.**

Duras: *Des Journées entières dans les arbres*, **1977.**

Duras: *Des Journées entières dans les arbres*, **1977.**

Duras: *Des Journées entières dans les arbres*, **1977.**

Duras: *Des Journées entières dans les arbres*, **1977.**

Duras: *Le Camion*, **1977.**

Duras: *Le Camion*, **1977.**

CONCLUSIONS

(By Way of a Flashback)

Six decades have passed since the first French literary figure (Guitry) took up the camera to put his vision on celluloid. Since the boulevardier's presound "talky," the wedding of these two careers by the pleiad presented here has engendered a checkered history ranging from dramatically appalling to intellectually appealing. Although the situation has ameliorated, among the professional filmmakers and certain critics there still exists a slight condescension toward littérateurs who are considered nonprofessional trespassers. This antagonism was originally felt because the *arrivistes* showed themselves short on technique, especially in their earliest films, as might be expected. It must be said, however, that the new breed of literary filmmakers was never wanting in imaginative ideas.

The battle has not completely subsided, however, and before long there will be more cinematic cadavers on the battlefield, for Marguerite Duras at Cannes launched a torpedo that for many caused irreparable damage to the rapport between cinema and literature. With the optimism of a Cassandra, Duras more than frankly stated that the cinema can go to rack and ruin, and that she was only interested in *another* type of cinema, as we have previously observed. At the same press conference one of the members of the audience in a not too gentle tone asked Duras how she could possibly film "such things." For ten years, she replied, she had to defend herself for her radical experimentation in film, and now she refuses to do so. That was the end of her response. At one of the showings of *Le Camion* she was booed and hissed. Film history is replete with daring pioneers who were considered abnormal, mad, or fakes. Duras will hold her own.

In reality, a *tabula rasa* has never been totally effected in the film career of Marguerite Duras or the others, since they each brought to his or her cinematic works an aesthetic and thematic outlook that proved advantageous for the already initiated public. The symbiotic relationship of the two disciplines can be a fertile arrangement.

Very rare once upon a time, the literary filmmakers—although not exactly legion today—have become more numerous. The director who has been the most significant catalyst in the combination of the two arts has been Alain Resnais. Even before Duras's *Hiroshima*, Resnais had collaborated with Jean Cayrol, who wrote the scenario for *Nuit et brouillard* based on his poetry re-creating the construction of the concentration camps in the 1930s. After his second project in scripting *Muriel* (1963), Cayrol codirected a film with Claude Durand entitled *Le Coup de grâce* (1964) and directed his own work, *Do Not Disturb or Ne pas déranger* (1970). In addition to Duras, Robbe-Grillet, and Cayrol, Resnais "inspired" another novelist/filmmaker, the Spanish-born Jorge Semprun.[1] After writing the screenplays for Resnais's *La Guerre est finie* (1965) and *Stavisky* (1973) and Costa-Gavras's *Z* (1969) and *L'Aveu* (1970), Semprun tried his hand at a documentary on the Spanish Civil War. In the genre of "film-witness" exemplified by *Le Chagrin et la pitié* and *Français, si vous saviez,* Semprun's *Les Deux Mémoires* (1973) offers a multiple perspective on the war pieced together from the souvenirs and reflections of the crisis, as it unfolds a series of double impressions: the young versus the old, the red versus the white, the exiled versus the resident, and the Republican versus the Phalangist. At one point Malraux is interviewed, and the novelist/propagandist describes the sociopolitical context of his optimistic, pro-Republican novel *L'Espoir* (1937). Among Resnais's French collaborators only Jacques Sternberg, novelist (*Un Jour ouvrable*), screenwriter (*Je t'aime, je t'aime*), and editor (*Magazine Littéraire*) has not entered the realm of film.[2]

In the wake of the success of *Orphée*, Jean Cocteau mentioned to André Fraigneau that Jean Genet (whom Sartre has since canonized with his work *Saint Genet: Comédien et martyr*) had made "a very beautiful film where he speaks a visual language without the least restriction."[3] The film was difficult to see, observed Cocteau. It was censored from the moment of its completion for almost twenty-five years before it was made accessible for distribution in avant-garde theater programs. Serge Daney's analysis of Genet's *Un Chant d'amour* (1950), evokes perhaps the ambiance of the voyeurism of Robbe-Grillet in its description of the two prisoners separated by a wall.[4] The critic speaks of three holes—one (almost imperceptible) in the partition between the two cells through which the inmates lovingly pass a piece of straw; the second, a peephole for the guard; and the third, the movie screen on which the spectator observes the guard's imposition of his own desires on the prisoners. Thirty years ago, the attorney Maurice Garçon, pleading the cause of Genet accused of theft, said to the court: "This thief that you wish to send to prison for the rest of his life will be one of the great authors of the French language."[5] Now, following upon the feeble attempts of several filmmakers to adapt such works as *Le Balcon* and *Les Bonnes*, the scandal erupting in his staging of *Les Paravents* at the Théâtre de France (with Malraux's blessing), and his brief liaison with the Black Panthers in the United States, notably at M.I.T., Genet himself has written a scenario for a film that he also intended to direct, *La Nuit venue*. Genet, as usual very reticent about his work, described the film as the adventures of a young Moroccan who discovers before him an old universe (Europe, France, Paris), which was already showing signs of crumbling.

In the same vein of controversial cinéastes, the Spanish-born Fernando Arrabal, who like other foreign playwrights of the "absurdist" tendency (Beckett, Adamov, Ionesco) found political, psychological, and literary emancipation in France, lets his fertile and at times perverse imagination go wild in his cinematic productions. Buñuel's shocking (for the period) antiestablishment film *L'Age d'or* could very well be compared to a congenial fairy tale when placed side by side with Arrabal's three films to date. From his novel *Baal-Babylone*, Arrabal first filmed *Viva la Muerte* in 1970 in Tunisia. The film shows the cinéaste haunted by the repercussions of the Spanish Civil War and by obsessions with his mother. The portrayal of brutalities of every variety and the highlighting of sexual perversions resulted in an almost three-month period of censorship in France before the work was eventually distributed.[6]

Continuing in the same imaginative and desecratory furrow, Arrabal made *J'irai comme un cheval fou* in 1973, interweaving the dual themes of the Oedipus complex and the redemption by "purity." In a few words the film can be labeled "lyrical scatology." The violent and sexual once again become magnified and take on archetypal proportions.[7] Soon afterwards, he embarked on another work with a Spanish flavor, *L'Arbre de Guernica* (1975), recalling the famous oak tree in the village bombed on 26 April 1937, in the midst of the Spanish Civil War. One scene in particular is very graphic, inspired from one of the many atrocities of the war—the exhuming and scattering of the coffins around the façade of a church. A la Buñuel, Arrabal imaginatively choreographs a group of children dancing around several coffins with the skeletons exposed and labeled, for example, "capitalists," "exploiters," and "Fascists." This shock type of cinema in Arrabal has its public and is not isolated, as can be witnessed in R. Franco's *Pascal Duarte*, where the hero in a Gidean *acte gratuit* fires his double-barrel shotgun point blank at his mother as easily as he does at his dog, and as efficiently and brutally as he knifes a horse for having thrown his wife. Only the mother's death was staged, obviously; the actual graphic and crude slaying of the horse and dog would have caused any anticruelty association to rise up in arms against the filmmaker.

In the collaboration of Samuel Beckett and Alan Schneider in *Film* (1965), it is difficult to discern where the role of the screenwriter Beckett ends and that of the director Schneider begins. The writer's involvement with the work could be considered a filmmaking venture, the cooperation was so intimate. Schneider casually recounts how Beckett ("Sam") conceived of this short twenty-two minute film with only one word, "Sssh":

> *Film* was a short film commissioned for Evergreen Theatre. The script appeared in the spring of 1963 as a fairly baffling when not downright inscrutable six-page outline. Along with pages of addenda in Sam's inimitable informal style: explanatory notes, a philosophical supplement, modest production suggestions, a series of hand-drawn diagrams. Involving, in cosmic detail, his principal characters, O and E, and the question of "perceivedness," the angle of immunity, and the essential principle that *esse est percipi*: to be is to be perceived. All composed with loving care, humor, sadness, and Sam's ever-present compassionate understanding of man's essential frailty. I loved it even when I wasn't completely sure what Sam meant. And I suddenly decided that my early academic training in physics and geometry was finally going to pay off in my directorial career.[8]

In July 1964, Beckett came to America to work with Alan Schneider, Buster Keaton, and Boris Kaufman on the production of the film. The scene is 1929. The elderly Keaton cryptically dashes down the street, into a house, up a flight of stairs, and into his room. Here he blots out all external reality—destroying a print of God the Father; letting out the cat; covering over the parrot cage, the goldfish bowl, and the mirror; and tearing up a set of photographs that link him with his past. Only in the very last few moments do we see Keaton's face with a black patch over his eye. Schematized in O and E, this study in perception evokes some of the Sartrean philosophy of the look ("le regard"). The film was not appreciated commercially as a work of Beckett's or Keaton's, and its philosophical message went unnoticed. Nonetheless it won a trilogy of prizes at Venice, Tours, and Oberhausen indicating its avant-garde contribution to the realm of cinema.

When Françoise Sagan published *Bonjour tristesse* the literary world expressed delightful surprise at the display of talent in this promising prodigy. Otto Preminger was quick to transpose this work for the screen in 1958 with Jean Seberg, David Niven, and Deborah Kerr in the principal roles. Other adaptations of Sagan's novels were soon to follow, including *Un Certain Sourire, Château en Suède, Aimez-vous Brahms?,* and *La Chamade.* For Claude Chabrol's *Landru* (1962), Sagan furnished the dialogues but kept her interests limited strictly to literature. In February 1975, she began to dabble in film, directing her first short film, *Encore un hiver*, in the Luxembourg Gardens in Paris. With her full-length film *Les Fougères bleues* (1977), she is one of the latest littérateurs to yield to the temptation of filming her own work, this time from a short story entitled *Les Yeux de soie* (1976). The press of June 1977, in discussing the *ménage à quatre* in the mountain chalet of *Les Fougères bleues,* immediately let fly at the debutante filmmaker a barrage of tepid critiques. Thomas Quinn Curtiss (*International Herald Tribune*) referred to it as a "papier-mâché drama," whereas Pierre Montaigne (*Le Figaro*) considered it "an exercise of a pupil whose master could very well be Anatol Litvak" (i.e., the director of *Aimez-vous Brahms?* and *The Night of the Generals*), and "an interminable mixed doubles of ping-pong in slow-motion."[9] Through it all, however, Sagan has remained faithful to Sagan, meriting for herself just the same a seat in the Cannes Film jury in 1979.

Robbe-Grillet, the acclaimed "theoretician" of the Nouveau Roman, was not the only one of the nontraditionalist novelists to take to the camera. From the group of littérateurs such as Nathalie Sarraute, Samuel Beckett, Michel Butor, Claude Simon, Robert Pinget, and Claude Ollier (with Jerome Lindon of Editions de Minuit as the literary Maecenas), Claude Simon next heard the Sirens of the "world of shadows." "Like the early Godard and Buñuel," Simon stated, "(I wish) to plow my own furrow and to discover a personal technique in cinematic expression."[10] Claiming (like Sagan) fidelity to the literary narrative, Simon intends to adapt his novel *La Route des Flandres* wherein the hero, during a night following World War II, recalls the hostilities and debacle of 1940.

Perhaps less internationally famous than his literary cinematic predecessors, Sébastien Japrisot (Jean-Baptiste Rossi) has been busy at work **on the sidelines, Japrisot wrote the scripts for Costa-Gavras's pre-Z work** *Compartiment tueurs* (1965) and for René Clément's *Le Passager de la pluie* (1969). After bringing to the screen in 1975 his first novel *Les mal partis*, Japrisot continues his literary and cinematic production with the scenario for *Toi,* in which five actresses offer completely different ideas of the same woman. Before *Toi* reaches the screen, Japrisot will have already filmed *Une Rose blanche peinte en rouge*, a narrative situated on two levels of the psychological and the adventurous, where he does not camouflage his interest in Lewis Carroll's *Alice in Wonderland.*

The list of littérateurs entering the ranks of the film directors multiplies daily. The little stellar pleiad of seven very diversified filmmakers has thus been expanding into a full-blown Milky Way. In succumbing to the temptation of eating the forbidden fruit, these intellectuals have lost their pristine literary innocence, but in the end they have gained in the knowledge of their aesthetic talents and limitations.

NOTES

Chapter 1: Jean Cocteau

1. For two fascinating studies of Paris in the 1920s see Janet Flanner, *Paris Was Yesterday* (New York: The Viking Press, 1972), and James Harding, *The Ox on the Roof* (London: Macdonald, 1972).

2. The death of the singer Edith Piaf preceded Cocteau's by several hours, and his last formal statement acknowledging his grief was made to the press at Milly-la-Forêt shortly before he himself died.

3. "Réponse de M. André Maurois au discours de M. Jean Cocteau," *Discours... tenu à l'Académie française... le jeudi 20 octobre 1955* (Paris: Institut de France, 1955), p. 35.

4. Jean Cocteau (to René Guilly, *Combat*, 3 July 1948) quoted in *Entretiens sur le cinématographe* (Paris: Pierre Belfond, 1973), p. 159.

5. Interview with André Fraigneau in 1951, quoted in *Entretiens*, p. 43.

6. Jean Cocteau, *Le Sang d'un poète* (Monaco: Ed. du Rocher, 1957), p. 25.

7. Jean Domarchi and Jean-Louis Laugier, "Entretien avec Jean Cocteau," *Cahiers du Cinéma*, no. 109 (July 1960), p. 18.

8. Jean Cocteau in an interview with Fraigneau, *Entretiens*, p. 26.

9. Jean Cocteau, "*La Belle et la bête,*" *L'Avant-Scène du Cinéma*, nos. 138-39 (July-September 1973): 12. Fantasies like *La Belle et la bête*, the stories of Perreault, and others in the Bibliothèque Rose fed the imagination of the young Jean Cocteau.

10. Jean Cocteau (in 1949), quoted in *Du Cinématographe* (Paris: Pierre Belfond, 1973), p. 25.

11. Claude Beylie, "Cocteau," *Anthologie du Cinéma*, no. 12 (February 1966): 82.

12. Cocteau (in 1948), *Du Cinématographe*, p. 25.

13. For a further development of the recurrent themes in the literature and cinema of Cocteau, see James J. Tomek, "Relationship of Literature and Film in Cocteau," *Dissertation Abstracts International* 35, no. 5 (November 1974): 3014-15A.

14. Rui Nogueira, *Melville on Melville* (London: Secker and Warburg, 1971), p. 38.

15. Jean Cocteau, *Orphée: Film* (Paris: Ed. de la Parade, 1950). For another film version of the Orpheus myth see Marcel Camus's *Orfeu Negro*.

16. Jean Cocteau, in an interview with Fraigneau, *Entretiens*, p. 85.

17. René Gilson, "*Le Testament d'Orphée*," *Jean Cocteau*, Coll. Cinéma d'aujourd'hui, no. 27 (Paris: Seghers, 1964), p. 131.

18. See Francis Steegmuller, *Cocteau: A Biography* (Boston: Little Brown and Co., 1970), p. 495.

19. Jean Cocteau presided at the festival of "Films maudits" in Biarritz in 1949, in the course of which a prize was awarded the American epic *Mourning becomes Electra.* He would later preside at Cannes for the 1953, 1954, and 1957 festivals.

20. "Discours à l'Académie française," p. 16.

21. Gilson, "*Le Testament d'Orphée*," p. 130.

22. Neal Oxenhandler, *Scandal and Parade: The Theatre of Jean Cocteau* (New Brunswick, N.J.: Rutgers University Press, 1957), p. 78.

23. Cocteau (in 1950), quoted in *Du Cinématographe*, p. 128.

24. Cocteau, interview with Fraigneau, quoted in *Entretiens*, p. 68.

25. *Ibid.*, p. 95.

26. Jean Cocteau, "The Cat That Walks by Itself," *The Listener* (BBC), no. 1301 (4 February 1954): 211-12.

27. Jean Cocteau, interview with Jeanine Delpich (1946), quoted in *Entretiens*, p. 147.

Chapter 2: Sacha Guitry

1. Janet Flanner, *Paris Was Yesterday* (New York: The Viking Press, 1972), p. XXIV.
2. Claude Gauteur, "Entretiens avec Sacha Guitry," *Image et Son*, no. 248 (March 1971): 11.
3. Ibid., p. 20.
4. François Mars, "Citizen Sacha," *Cahiers du Cinéma*, no. 88. (October 1958): 22.
5. Jacques Siclier, "Sacha Guitry," *Anthologie du Cinéma*, no. 13 (March 1966): 120.
6. Louis Marcorelles, "Sacha Guitry," *Sight and Sound*, no. 2 (Autumn 1957): 101.
7. Siclier, "Sacha Guitry," p. 157.
8. François Gir, "Guitry au travail, par ses collaborateurs," *Cahiers du Cinéma*, no. 173 (December 1965): 97.
9. "La voix du maître: entretien avec Stéphane Prince," *Cahiers du Cinéma*, no. 173 (December 1965): 94.
10. Marcorelles, "Sacha Guitry" p. 101. For published memoirs that capture the creative Guitry in context, see Alexis Madis, *Sacha* (Paris: Ed. de l'Elan, 1950) and Jacques Lorcey, *Sacha Guitry: raconté par les témoins de sa vie* (Paris: Ed. France Empire, 1976).

Chapter 3: Marcel Pagnol

1. (Yvan Audouard), *Yvan Audouard raconte Pagnol* (Paris: Ed. Stock, 1973), p. 104.
2. Consult the address of Marcel Pagnol in *Discours prononcés dans la séance publique tenue par l'Académie française pour la réception de M. Marcel Pagnol* (Paris: Institut de France, 1947), p. 23. Audouard (p. 104) recounts the favorable impression that Pagnol made upon the Immortals: When Pagnol came to make the customary visit to the Academicians prior to his election, he told clever stories all the time, never spoke of his candidacy, and then simply left. He certainly was invited back, said François Mauriac.
3. André Bazin, "Théâtre et cinéma," *Esprit*, no. 180 (June 1951): 891. More successful in "filmed theater" was the German expressionist cinema with Wiene's *Dr. Caligari's Cabinet* as a graphic example of expanding the limits of the physical stage.
4. André Bazin, "Le Cas Pagnol," *Qu'est-ce que le Cinéma?*, vol. 2 (Paris: Ed. du Cerf, 1959), pp. 119-25.
5. Cf. "Dossier: Marcel Pagnol (1895-1974)," *Magazine Littéraire*, no. 99 (April 1975): 7.
6. Claude Beylie, *Marcel Pagnol*, Coll. Cinéma d'aujourd'hui, 80 (Paris: Seghers, 1974), p. 18.
7. Pierre Leprohon, "Marcel Pagnol," *Anthologie du Cinéma*, no. 88 (May 1976): 391.
8. Jean-André Fieschi, Gérard Guégan, Jacques Rivette, "Une aventure de la parole," *Cahiers du Cinéma*, no. 173 (December 1965): 27.
9. Leprohon, "Marcel Pagnol," p. 395.
10. "*Cigalon*," *L'Avant-Scène du Cinéma*, nos. 105-6 (July-September 1970): 103-10.
11. "*Le Schpountz*," *L'Avant-Scène du Cinéma*, nos. 105-6 (July-September 1970): 3-87.
12. Marcel Pagnol, *Le Château de ma mère: Souvenirs d'Enfance* (2) (Paris: Ed. de Provence, 1958).
13. Georges Berni, *Marcel Pagnol: Enfant d'Aubagne et de La Treille* (Aubagne: Artigot Press, 1977), illustration between pp. 17 and 18.
14. Quoted in *L'Avant-Scène*, nos. 105-6, p. 7.
15. Audouard, *Yvan Audouard*, p. 133.
16. Gérard Perron, "Albert Dubout: Affichiste de cinéma," *Lumière*, no. 1 (February 1977): 39-47.
17. Gaston Bonheur, "La Gloire de Pagnol," *Paris-Match* (May 1976), p. 80. See also Pierre Leprohon, "Raimu," *Anthologie du cinéma*, no. 42 (February 1969): 51-104.
18. Bonheur, "La Gloire de Pagnol," p. 74.
19. Bazin, "Le Cas Pagnol," p. 119.
20. Pierre Montaigne, "Du néo-réalisme de *Rome, ville ouverte* au cinéma didactique du *Messie*: L'itinéraire de Roberto Rossellini," *Le Figaro*, 4-5 June 1977, p. 30.

21. See this testimony in Jean-André Fieschi et al., p. 27, and Patrick Brion, "L'inventeur du néo-réalisme," *Magazine Littéraire*, no. 99 (April 1975): 12-14.

22. Beylie, *Marcel Pagnol*, p. 159.

23. Audouard, *Yvan Audouard*, p. 220. For another eulogy of Pagnol the tale-teller, see Claude Roy's "La saga des garriques," *Le Nouvel Observateur*, no. 656 (6 June 1977): 70, where Roy refers to Pagnol as truly a *popular* writer in the pure, etymological sense of the word, classifying him somewhere between Robert Louis Stevenson and Mark Twain.

Chapter 4: Jean Giono

1. (Yvan Audouard), *Yvan Audouard raconte Pagnol* (Paris: Ed. Stock, 1973), p. 60.

2. Pierre Leprohon, *Présences contemporaines: Cinéma* (Paris: Ed. Debresse, 1957), pp. 217-18.

3. Six interviews with Pagnol were shown on French television in 1973 and 1975. The fifth session discussed the Pagnol/Giono collaboration in some detail.

4. Jean Giono, *Solitude de la pitié*, in *Oeuvres Romanesques*, Coll. La Pleiad, vol. 1 (Paris: Gallimard, 1971), pp. 491-501. References to the novels and short stories published in this edition are given the abbreviation *OR*, with the volume and pagination.

5. In Claude Beylie's *Marcel Pagnol*, see especially Chapter VIII, "Giono revisité."

6. Marcel Pagnol, *Jofroi* in *Oeuvres Complètes*, vol. 4 (Paris: Ed. de Provence, 1968), pp. 339-99. Further references to the complete works of Pagnol are indicated as *OC*.

7. Scotto ordinarily composed the music for Pagnol's films, but in this case he also agreed to play a role in *Jofroi*. In 1950 he won an Oscar for his acting in the film; he did not act in any further productions of Pagnol.

8. For this aesthetic parallel consult the photographs in the article by Claude Gauteur, "Giono et le cinéma," *Magazine Littéraire*, no. 75 (April 1973): 24.

9. Jean-Pierre Grenier, *Jofroi—d'après Giono* (Grenoble: Ed. Les Françaises Nouvelles, 1943).

10. Giono, *OR*, vol. 1, p. 964.

11. Jean Giono, *Un de Baumugnes* (Paris: Grasset, 1929). Also published in *OR*, vol. 1, pp. 219-319.

12. Fernandel's acting in *Angèle* explains the success of the film. On the talent of this comedian, read "Adieu Fernandel," *Ciné Revue*, no. 10 (11 March 1971): 29-31.

13. Giono, *OR*, vol. 1, pp. 323-429.

14. Jean Giono, "Préface de *Regain*," Coll. Les Films qu'on peut lire (Paris/Marseille: Ed. Marcel Pagnol, 1937), p. 157.

15. Ibid., pp. 163-187. Here Pagnol recounts a long series of anecdotes dealing with the filming of *Regain*.

16. Jean Giono, "Le Boulanger, le berger, Aurélie," *Jean le Bleu* (Paris: Grasset, 1932), pp. 173-90. Also in *OR*, vol. 1 pp. 100-115.

17. Marcel Pagnol, *La Femme du boulanger*, in *OC*, vol. 6 (Paris: Ed. de Provence, 1973), p. 20. See also Giono's *La Femme du boulanger* in *Théâtre de Jean Giono* (Paris: Gallimard, 1943), pp. 195-346.

18. Several members of the clergy were upset by Pagnol's "caricature" of the curate. The director justified his treatment of this personage in a letter to M. l'Abbé Chamonin, editor of *Le Courrier de Genève*, dated 24 September 1938. On television Pagnol said he grew up in an educationally oriented family that was basically anticlerical, hence some of the inspiration for the material in the film came right out of the existential situation.

19. Alexandre Arnoux and Roger Regent, "Ils vous parlent de Raimu," *L'Ecran français*, No. 325 (3-9 October 1951), pp. 11-17, 22. Orson Welles once spoke of Raimu as one of the greatest actors on the international scene.

20. C. E. J. Caldicott, "Notice bibliographique et judiciaire sur la collaboration de Jean Giono avec Marcel Pagnol," *Revue de l'Université d'Ottawa* 41, no. 4 (October-December 1971): 563-566.

21. Michel Grisolia, "Giono: un homme de la Renaissance (Entretien avec Jean Carrière)," *Magazine Littéraire*, no. 75 (April 1973): 18.

22. Jean Giono, "Le Bout de la route," *Les Cahiers du Contadour*, no. 2 (1937). Also in *Théâtre de Jean Giono*, pp. 7-101.

23. Jacques Gambier Laforterie, "Le Hussard dans le tiroir," *France Film, Cinéma Nouveau*, no. 19 (March-May 1962): 4.

24. François Villiers, "Un symbolisme discret," in "Cinq jeunes cinéastes français," *Cahiers du Cinéma*, no. 83 (May 1958): 29.

25. Claude Mauriac, "Le Cinéma: *L'Eau vive," Le Figaro Littéraire*, no. 636 (28 June 1958): 18.

26. Jean Giono and Alain Allioux, *Hortense ou l'eau vive* (Paris: France-Empire, 1958). The film deals with the text found on pp. 99-301.

27. In Claudine Chonez' *Giono par lui-même* (Paris: Ed. du Seuil, 1956), p. 62, we can see the author's historical documentation on cholera, and on pp. 168-69, the itinerary through certain zones of cholera in *Le Hussard sur le toit*.

28. W. D. Redfern, *The Private World of Jean Giono* (Oxford: Basil Blackwell, 1967). On p. 179, Redfern discusses briefly the purifying effect of fire during the epic in the film when candles, prayers, and curses have failed.

29. From the scenario of *Le Foulard de Smyrne*, a photocopy of which was kindly offered to me in 1975 by Mlle. Aline Giono along with other invaluable details. The scenario has since been published in *Bulletin des Amis de Jean Giono*, no. 6 (Autumn/Winter 1975).

30. In 1959, *La Duchesse* merited a prize in the short film category at the Brussels Film Festival.

31. François Villiers, "Hommage à Giono," *Le Figaro Littéraire*, no. 1274 (19-25 October 1970): p. 19.

32. "*Crésus*: Un film de Jean Giono," *Arts*, 27 April 1960, p. 5. The film was presented for the annual Giono session at Manosque on 29 July 1977.

33. Jean Giono, *Crésus: Livre de conduite du metteur en scène, indications, techniques et dialogues* (Manosque: Ricco, 1961).

34. Gauteur, "Giono et le cinéma," p. 21.

35. Jean Giono, *Les Grands Chemins* (Paris: Gallimard, 1948).

36. Jean Giono, *Un Roi sans divertissement* (Paris: Gallimard, 1948). Also in *OR*, vol. 3 pp. 453-606.

37. The scenario is found in the appendix of *OR*, vol. 3, pp. 1340-96.

38. Odile de Pomerai, "A Novelist Turns to Films: Jean Giono and the Cinema," *Twentieth Century Literature* 12 no. 2 (July 1966): 59-65. Although this article does not mention several films drawn from Giono's works and lacks certain significant details on Giono's affiliation with the cinema, it does represent the most sensitive and elaborate work to this date on the adaptation of *Un Roi sans divertissement*.

39. At the Chicago Film Festival of 1964, the film was awarded a First Prize.

40. Jean Collet, "Magie de Giono: *Un Roi sans divertissement," Le Signe du Temps*, no. 1 (October 1963): 39.

41. Jean Giono, *Le Chant du monde* (Paris: Gallimard, 1934). Also in *OR*, vol. 2, pp 187-412.

42. The untamed river and the savage country overridden by the inhabitants' barbaric spirit also serve as decor for the American film *Deliverance*.

43. André Besseges, "Ce qu'ils réalisent après *Orfeu Negro," France Catholique*, 24 September 1965).

44. W. D. Redfern, "*Le Chant du monde:* roman pur," *Nouvelle Revue Française*, no. 218 (February 1971): 36.

45. From the minutes of the meeting of the Chamber of Commerce in Digne, held at Manosque on 12 January 1966, with Jean Giono and M. Serrin present to discuss the project. I am grateful to the Chamber of Commerce for the extensive documents provided for the research on this film.

46. A film on Jean Giono entitled *Manosque* was directed by Georges Regnier in 1942 and another by Pierre Gout, *Jean Giono*, filmed sometime in the 1950s.

47. From a letter of M. Pico, president of the Chamber of Commerce at Digne to his colleagues, dated 24 January 1966.

48. Alain Boudet completed *Le Déserteur* in 1973, based on Giono's narrative of the life of the enigmatic artist Charles-Frédéric Brun in Switzerland in the 1800s. *Le Hussard sur le toit, Jean le Bleu*, and *Les Récits de la demi-brigade* have been discussed in terms of television adaptations, but further details were unavailable.

Chapter 5: André Malraux

1. For this testimony see *L'Express*, no. 1325 (29 November-5 December 1976) and *Les Nouvelles Littéraires*, no. 2560 (25 November-1 December 1976).

2. Jean Arc'houan, "Malraux: la part de l'imposture." *Les Ecrits de Paris,* March 1977, pp. 49-53.

3. André Malraux, *Le Métamorphose des dieux: L'Intemporel*, (Paris: Gallimard, 1976). For cinematic references see pages 84, 89, 368-69, 371, 381, and 403.

4. Renaud Matignon, "A 2: *Espoir* au ciné-club: Au carrefour de l'histoire," *Le Figaro*, 26 November 1976, p. 31.

5. Two works that discuss Malraux's early cinematic interest may be signaled here: André Vandégans, *La Jeunesse littéraire d'André Malraux* (Paris: Pauvert, 1964) and Franz J. Albersmeir, *André Malraux und der Film: Zur Rezeption des Films in Frankreich* (Bern: Herbert Lang, 1973).

6. André Malraux, *Esquisse d'une psychologie du cinéma* (Paris: Gallimard, 1946).

7. Quoted in *L'Humanité*, no. 10.034 (24 November 1976), p. 11.

8. See the "Dossier-film" of *Sierra de Teruel* established by Marcel Oms in *Les Cahiers de la Cinémathèque*, no. 21 (January 1977): 57-66.

9. For Ivens' objectives see in the same edition of *Les Cahiers de la Cinémathèque*, "Dossier-film: *Terre d'Espagne*," p. 39.

10. It is impossible to obtain an accurate, historical picture of the actual filming of *Espoir* without the documents of Max Aub in Malraux's *Sierra de Teruel* (Mexico City: Ed. Era, 1968) and Denis Marion, *André Malraux*, Coll. Cinéma d'aujourd'hui (Paris: Seghers, 1970).

11. The pagination is from André Malraux's *L'Espoir* in *Romans* (Paris: Gallimard, 1947). The schema is an abbreviated version of this author's work, *André Malraux's Espoir: The Art/Propaganda Film in the Spanish Civil War* (University, Miss.: Romance Language Monographs, 1977), pp. 38-43.

12. Marion, *André Malraux*, p. 42.

13. Bertolt Brecht, *Journal du travail: 1938-1955* (Paris: L'Arche, 1977), p. 446.

14. André Malraux, "The Fascist Threat to Culture," Harvard University Address (8 March 1937), trans. by Ethel Saniel.

15. Pierre Galante, *Malraux: Quel roman que sa vie* (Paris: Plon, 1971), p. 161.

16. The propaganda film has recently been treated in two works: Roy P. Madsen, *The Impact of Film* (New York: Macmillan Publishing Co., 1973) and Leif Furhammer and Folke Isaksson, *Politics and Film*, trans. by Kersti French (New York: Praeger Publishers, 1971).

17. For several different perspectives on Guernica see the films of Robert Flaherty, Alain Resnais, and Fernando Arrabal.

18. Quoted in *Les Cahiers de la Cinémathèque*, no. 21, p. 21.

19. From the publicity materials distributed at the rerelease of *Espoir* in 1970.

20. See Joris Ivens, *The Camera and I* (New York: International Publications, 1969), and the article "Dossier-film: *Terre d'Espagne*," in *Les Cahiers de la Cinémathèque*, no. 21, pp. 35-41.

21. Carlos F. Cuenca, *La Guerra de España y el cine*, 2 vols. (Madrid, Ed. Nationale, 1972).

22. Pierre Lhermier, *L'Art du cinéma* (Paris: Seghers, 1960), pp. 13-14.

23. Marcel Martin, "André Malraux," *Ecran*, no. 54 (15 January 1977): 74.

Chapter 6: Alain Robbe-Grillet

1. Alain Robbe-Grillet, "Mes Romans et mes films," *Magazine Littéraire*, no. 6 (April 1967): 13. (Interview with Jean-Jacques Brochier.)

2. Alain Robbe-Grillet, *L'Année dernière à Marienbad* (Paris: Ed. de Minuit, 1961). *Marienbad* is considered here as an original conception of Robbe-Grillet, although Resnais directed the film. As with *L'Immortelle*, the purpose of a *ciné-roman* is to provide a facile base for studying the work in greater detail, a difficult task during the projection of the film.

3. André Labarthe and Jacques Rivette, "Entretien avec Resnais et Robbe-Grillet," *Cahiers du Cinéma*, no. 123 (September 1961): 2.

4. André Gardies, *Alain Robbe-Grillet*, Coll. Cinéma d'aujourd'hui, no. 70 (Paris: Ed. Seghers, 1972), p. 125. This is the most comprehensive work to date on Robbe-Grillet as a filmmaker. Gardies also participated in the "Colloque de Cerisy" the proceedings of which are published in two volumes in the collection 10/18 (Union Générale d'Editions. 1976).

5. Gardies, *Alain Robbe-Grillet*, p. 148.

6. Penelope Houston, "Resnais/Antonioni: *L'Année dernière à Marienbad* and *La Notte,*" *Sight and Sound*, no. 1 (Winter 1961-62): 28.

7. Jacques Doniol-Valcroze, "Istanbul nous appartient," *Cahiers du Cinéma*, no. 143 (May 1963): 55.

8. Alain Robbe-Grillet, *Glissements progressifs du plaisir* (Paris: Ed. de Minuit, 1974), p. 147.

9. Jacques Brunius, "Every year at Marienbad," *Sight and Sound*, no. 3 (Summer 1962): 124.

10. Robbe-Grillet, *Glissements*, p. 148.

11. Anne Mason and Michel Dunois, "Rencontre avec Robbe-Grillet, un vrai compliqué," *L'Aurore*, no. 7972 (18-19 April 1970): 2.

12. Gardies, *Alain Robbe-Grillet*, p. 155.

13. For a further development of the topic of *chosisme*, see Jean Alter, "Alain Robbe-Grillet and the 'cinematic style,' " *Modern Language Journal*, no. 6 (October 1964): 365.

14. Gardies, *Alain Robbe-Grillet*, p. 55.

15. Michel Capdenac, "Alain Robbe-Grillet: Le jeu de l'aventure, du mythe et de l'amour," *Les Lettres Françaises*, no. 1167 (27 January 1967), p. 18.

16. Alain Robbe-Grillet, "Après *L'Eden et après,*" *Nouvel Observateur*, no. 294 (29 June 1970) p. 34.

17. Pierre Montaigne, "Robbe-Grillet entre la foudre et l'encens," *Le Figaro* (18 February 1975), p. 24. Robbe-Grillet said at Cerisy that he is very conscious of using the Bible for inspiration: Cf. for example, *TEE* with characters Matthieu, Lucette, Marc and Jean; and *Eden*'s reference to Genesis.

18. Alain Robbe-Grillet, "Le mot du metteur en scène: Jeux de l'initiation," *Le Figaro* (15 April 1970), p. 30.

19. Gardies, *Alain Robbe-Grillet*, p. 146.

20. C(olette) G(odard), "Robbe-Grillet et le mythe de la cover girl," *Le Monde*, no. 9367 (26 February 1975), p. 23.

21. *Glissements* and Marguerite Duras's *Baxter, Vera Baxter* could very well serve as subsequent panels for the Italian film *The Sorceresses* (1966), made by F. Rossi, M. Bolognini, P. Pasolini, L. Visconti, and V. de Sica.

22. Pierre Montaigne, "Robbe-Grillet" p. 24.

Chapter 7: Marguerite Duras

1. Marguerite Duras, *Un Barrage contre le Pacifique* (Paris: Gallimard, 1958), pp. 162-63.

2. For a more complete list of women filmmakers in France see the article "Mesdames les réalisatrices," *Cinéma Français*, no. 2 (June 1976): 13-16.

3. Xavière Gauthier, *Les Parleuses* (Paris: Ed. de Minuit, 1974). Duras's interviewer, although trying to pigeonhole the artist as a feminist, manages to get at the heart of many key issues in a very extensive interview. At a press conference in Cannes (1977), Marguerite Duras insisted that she goes *beyond* the feminist movement in her works.

4. Michel Delahaye, "Un entretien avec Resnais," *Cinéma '59*, no. 38 (July 1959): 1-3. The collaboration of Resnais with Duras would be one of many that he would undertake, as is seen in the conclusions.

5. Marguerite Duras, "Travailler pour le cinéma," *France-Observateur*, no. 430 (31 July 1958), p. 20.

6. Jean Domarchi, "Cannes 1960," *Cahiers du Cinéma*, no. 108 (June 1960), pp. 41-42.

7. Dionys Mascolo, "Naissance de la tragédie," *Marguerite Duras*, Coll. Ca/Cinéma (Paris: Ed. Albatros, 1975), p. 110.

8. Nicole Lise Bernheim, *Marguerite Duras tourne un film*, Coll. Ça/Cinéma (Paris: Albatros, 1974), p. 104.

9. Marguerite Duras, "La femme d'Evreux," *Cahiers du Cinéma*, no. 187 (February 1967): 43. Séban has profited from this exposure to the literary aspect of film and presented at Cannes (1977) an example of *théâtre filmé* with *Cathérine* adapted from Louis Aragon's *Les Cloches de Bâle*.

10. Gauthier, *Les Parleuses*, p. 200.

11. Fernard Dufour. "Nathalie Granger," *Cinéma 73*, no. 181 (November 1973): 126-127.

12. Gauthier, *Les Parleuses*, p. 77.

13. Jean-Louis Barrault, "Entretien avec Marguerite Duras," *Cahiers Renaud/Barrault*, no. 91 (1976): 6.

14. Vincent Canby, "Marguerite Duras's *India Song*, a Four-Hankie Story," *New York Times*, 8 October 1975, p. 24.

15. From a statement made in the press release and press conference 21 May 1977: "Que le cinéma aille à sa perte, c'est le seul cinéma. Que le monde aille à sa perte, qu'il aille à sa perte, c'est la seule politique." For a long interview on *Le Camion* and *Baxter, Vera Baxter*, see Jacques Grant and Jacques Frenais. "Marguerite Duras: Un acte contre tout pouvoir," *Cinéma 77*, no. 223 (July 1977): 48-58.

16. For an extensive and thematic study of Duras' work, especially of a literary nature, see Alain Vircondelet, *Marguerite Duras ou le temps de détruire*, Coll. Ecrivains d'hier et d'aujourd'hui (Paris: Seghers, 1972).

17. Bernheim, *Marguerite Duras tourne un film*, p. 41.

18. Vircondelet, *Marguerite Duras*, p. 91.

19. Duras, *Un Barrage conte le Pacifique*, p. 252.

20. Maguerite Duras, "*Détruire dit-elle*: La destruction, la parole," *Cahiers du Cinéma*, no. 217 (November 1969): 51.

21. Marguerite Duras, *India Song: Texte-Théâtre-Film* (Paris: Gallimard, 1973), p. 9. Even the geographical names are meant to be musical in this film.

22. Jack Gouseland, "Le feu d'artifice de Marguerite Duras," *Le Point*, no. 230 (14 February 1977): 84.

23. Vircondelet, *Marguerite Duras*, p. 54.

24. Duras, "*Détruire dit-elle*: La destruction, la parole," p. 52 ff.

25. Gauthier, *Les Parleuses*, p. 23.

26. Marguerite Duras, "*Des Journées entières dans les arbres:* Mothers," *Le Monde*, no. 9963 (10 February 1977): 17.

27. Jean de Baroncelli, "*Des Journées entières dans les arbres* de M. Duras," *Le Monde*, no. 9967 (15 February 1977), p. 23. For the mother-daughter relationship see *Hiroshima, Nathalie Granger*, and *Le Camion*.

28. Marguerite Duras, "Hiroshima... notre amour,"*Cahiers libres de la Jeunesse*, no. 1 (15 February 1960): 17.

29. Gilles Jacob, *Cinéma Moderne* (SERDOC: Lyons, 1964), pp. 225-26.

Conclusions

1. In March 1977, during the course of an interview with Alain Resnais on *Providence*, the director remarked to us that he did not launch these novelists into cinema, nor specifically assist them in their careers, but he felt that they greatly appreciated the intricacies of the film industry after their contact with him.

2. David Mercer, British playwright and scriptwriter (*Family Life* of Ken Loach), is the most recent collaborator of Resnais with his controversial literary contribution for *Providence*.

3. Jean Cocteau, (René Guilly, *Combat*, 3 July 1948) quoted in *Entretiens sur la cinématographe*, pp. 35-36.

4. Serge Daney, "*Un Chant d'amour* (Genet)," *Cahiers du Cinéma*, no. 264 (February 1976): 60.

5. Quoted by Pierre Montaigne in "Jean Genet cinéaste et metteur en scène,' *Le Figaro*, 3 February 1977, p. 25.

6. Fernando Arrabal, "*Viva la Muerte*," *L'Avant-Scène du Cinéma*, no. 116 (July 1971). Prior to this film, in 1968, Arrabal allowed Pierre-Alain Jolivet to adapt his play *Le Grand Cérémonial* (1966).

7. Mireille Amiel, *"J'irai comme un Cheval fou," Cinéma '74*, no. 183 (January 1974); 108-9.

8. Alain Schneider, "On Directing *Film," Film* (New York: Grove Press, 1969), p. 65.

9. Thomas Quinn Curtiss, "Paris Films: Sagan Takes Plunge into Movie Medium," *International Herald Tribune*, 8 June 1977, p. 5, and Pierre Montaigne, *"Les Fougères bleues:* Sagan fidèle à Sagan," *Le Figaro* (4-5 June 1977), p. 27.

10. Pierre Montaigne, "Claude Simon: du stylo à la caméra," *Le Figaro*, 12-13 February 1977, p. 19.

FILMOGRAPHY

Jean Cocteau: 1889-1963

1925 Direction of *Jean Cocteau fait du cinéma* (16 mm).

1930 Direction of *Le Sang d'un poète.*

1940 Adaptation and dialogues for *La Comédie du bonheur*, from a play by Nicolas Evreïnoff, directed by Marcel L'Herbier.

1942 Dialogues for *Le Baron fantôme*, with scenario and direction by Serge de Poligny.

1943 Scenario and dialogues for *L'Eternel Retour*, directed by Jean Delannoy.

1945 Dialogues for *Les Dames du Bois de Boulogne*, adapted from Diderot's *Jacques le fataliste*, and directed by Robert Bresson.

1946 Script, dialogues, and direction of *La Belle et la bête*, with technical assistance of René Clément.

Commentary for *L'Amitié noire*, directed by François Villiers and G. Krull.

1947 Scenario and dialogues for *Ruy Blas*, from Hugo's dramatic work, directed by Pierre Billon.

Scenario, dialogues, and direction of *L'Aigle à deux têtes*, with technical assistance of Hervé Bromberger.

1948 Original play of *La Voix humaine*, adapted by Roberto Rossellini in *L'Amore.*

Commentary written and spoken for *Les Noces de sable*, directed by André Zwoboda.

Commentary for *La Légende de Sainte Ursule*, directed by Luciano Emmer.

1948 Dialogues and direction of *Les Parents terribles.*

1950 Scenario and dialogues for *Les Enfants terribles*, directed by Jean-Pierre Melville.

Scenario, dialogues, and direction of *Orphée.*

Commentary written and spoken for *Venise et ses amants*, directed by Luciano Emmer and Enrico Gras.

Direction of *Coriolan* (16 mm).

1951 Commentary for French version of *Le Rossignol de l'Empire de Chine* (marionettes), directed by Jiri Trinka.

1952 Direction of *La Villa Santo-Sospir*, with the assistance of Frédéric Rossif.

Scenario for *La Couronne noire*, directed by Luis Saslavski.

1953 Commentary for *Le Rouge est mis*, directed by Igor Barrère and Hubert Knapp.

1956 Commentary for *A l'aube d'un monde*, directed by René Lucot. Preface for *Pantomimes*, directed by Paul Paviot with Marcel Marceau.

1957 Original play of *Le Bel Indifférent*, directed by Jacques Demy.

1958 Improvisation in a sketch for *Le Musée Grévin*, directed by Jacques Demy and Jean Masson.

1960 Scenario, dialogues, and direction of *Le Testament d'Orphée ou Ne me demandez pas pourquoi.*

1961 Adaptation and dialogues for *La Princesse de Clèves* of Mme de la Fayette, directed by Jean Delannoy.

1963 Original play of *Anna la Bonne*, adapted by Claude Jutra with music of Cocteau.

1965 Adaptation of his own novel *Thomas l'Imposteur* (with Georges Franju and Michel Worm), directed by Georges Franju.

Sacha Guitry: 1885-1957

1915 Direction of *Ceux de chez nous.*

1924 Original play of *The Lover of Camille (Debureau)*, adapted by Granville Barker and directed by Harry Beaumont.

1930 Original play of *Sleeping Partners (Faisons un rêve)*, directed by Seymour Hicks.

1931 Scenario, dialogues, for *Le Blanc et le noir*, directed by Robert Florey.

1935 Original play *Les Deux Couverts*, directed by Léonce Perret.
Scenario, dialogues, and direction of *Pasteur.*
Scenario, dialogues, and direction of *Bonne Chance.*

1936 Scenario, dialogues, and direction of *Le Roman d'un tricheur.*
Scenario, dialogues, and direction of *Le Nouveau Testament.*
Scenario, dialogues, and direction of *Mon père avait raison.*
Scenario, dialogues, and direction of *Faisons un rève.*
Scenario, dialogues, and direction of *Le Mot de Cambronne.*

1937 Scenario and dialogues for *Les Perles de la couronne*, directed by Guitry and Christian Jaque.
Scenario, dialogues, and direction of Désiré.
Scenario, dialogues, and direction of *Quadrille.*

1938 Scenario and dialogues for *L'Accroche-coeur*, directed by Pierre Caron.
Scenario, dialogues, and direction of *Remontons les Champs-Elysées.*

1939 Scenario, dialogues, and direction of *Ils étaient neuf célibataires.*

1940 Original play of *Lucky Partners* (remake of *Bonne Chance*, 1935), directed by Lewis Milestone.

1941 Scenario, dialogues, and direction of *Le Destin fabuleux de Désirée Clary.*

1942 Direction of *La Nuit du cinéma*.

1943 Scenario, dialogues, and direction of *Donne-moi tes yeux*.
Scenario, dialogues, and direction of *La Malibran*.

1947 Scenario, dialogues, and direction of *Le Comédien*.

1948 Scenario, dialogues, and direction of *Le Diable boiteux*.

1949 Scenario, dialogues, and direction of *Aux Deux Colombes*.
Scenario, dialogues, and direction of *Toa*.
Scenario, dialogues, and direction of *Le Trésor de Cantenac*.

1950 Scenario, dialogues, and direction of *Tu m'as sauvé la vie*.
Scenario, dialogues, and direction of *Debureau*.

1951 Scenario and dialogues for *Adhémar ou Le Jouet de la fatalité*, directed by Fernandel.
Scenario, dialogues, and direction of *La Poison*.

1952 Scenario, dialogues, and direction of *Je l'ai été trois fois*.
Scenario, dialogues, and direction of *La Vie d'un honnête homme*.

1953 Scenario, dialogues, and direction of *Si Versailles m'était conté*.

1954 Scenario, dialogues, and direction of *Napoléon*.

1955 Scenario, dialogues, and direction of *Si Paris nous était conté*.

1956 Scenario, dialogues, and direction of *Assassins et voleurs*.

1957 Scenario and dialogues for *Les Trois font la paire*, co-directed by Guitry and Clément Duhour.

1958 Scenario and dialogues, for *La Vie à deux* (before his death), directed by Clément Duhour.

Marcel Pagnol: 1895-1974

1931 Scenario and dialogues for *Marius*, directed by Alexander Korda.

1932 Scenario and dialogues for *Fanny*, directed by Marc Allégret.

1933 Original play of *Topaze*, adapted by Léopold Marchand and directed (first version) by Louis Gasnier.
Original play of Pagnol and Paul Nivoix *Un Direct au coeur*, directed by Roger Lion.
Scenario and dialogues, of *L'Agonie des aigles* from the novel *Les Demi-Soldes* of Georges d'Esparbès, directed by Roger Richebé.
Scenario and dialogues of *Léopold le bien-aimé*, co-directed by Pagnol and Charles Brun.

1934 Scenario, dialogues, and direction of *Le Gendre de Monsieur Poirier*, from the play of Emile Augier and Jules Sandeau.
Scenario, dialogues, and direction of *Jofroi*, from Giono's "Jofroi de la Maussan."
Scenario, dialogues, and direction of *L'Article 300*, from the play of Georges Courteline.
Scenario, dialogues, and direction of *Angèle*, from Giono's *un de Baumugnes*.
Scenario and dialogues for *Tartarin de Tarascon*, from the novel of Alphonse Daudet, directed by Raymond Bernard.

1935 Scenario, dialogues, and direction of *Merlusse*.
Scenario, dialogues, and direction of *Cigalon*.

1936 Scenario, dialogues, and direction of *César*.
Scenario, dialogues, and direction of *Topaze* (2nd version).

1937 Scenario, dialogues, and direction of *Regain* from Giono's novel.

1938 Scenario, dialogues, and direction of *Le Schpountz*.
Scenario, dialogues, and direction of *La Femme du boulanger* from an episode of Giono's "Jean le bleu."

1939 Scenario and dialogues for *Monsieur Brotonneau*, from the play of Robert de Flers and Gaston Arman de Caillavet, directed by Alexandre Esway.

1940 Scenario, dialogues, and direction of *La Fille du puisatier*.

1945 Scenario, dialogues, and direction of *Naïs*, from the short story of Emile Zola, "Naïs Micoulin," directed by Raymond Lenoursier, supervised by Pagnol.

1948 Scenario, dialogues, and direction of *La Belle Meunière*.

1950 Scenario, dialogues, and direction of *Le Rosier de Madame Husson*, from the short story of de Maupassant, directed by Jean Boyer.

1951 Scenario, dialogues, and direction of *Topaze* (3rd version).

1952 Scenario, dialogues, and direction of *Manon des Sources*.

1953 Scenario and dialogues for *Carnaval*, from Emile Mazaud's play, Dardamelle, directed by Henri Verneuil.

1954 Scenario, dialogues, and direction of *Les Lettres de mon moulin* from Daudet's tales.

1956 Original play of *Topaze* (TV version), directed by Jean Kerchbron.

1962 Scenario and dialogues for *La Dame aux camélias* (TV version) from Alexandre Dumas's play, directed by François Gir.

1965 Original play of *Merlusse* (TV version), directed by Georges Folgoas.

1967 Scenario and dialogues of *Le Curé de Cucugnan* (TV version) from Daudet's tale.

1975 Original scenario of *Cigalon* (TV version), directed by Georges Folgoas.

Jean Giono: 1895-1970

1933 Original story of *Jofroi* from "Jofroi de la Maussan" directed by Pagnol.

1934 Original novel of *Angèle* from *Un de Baumugnes*, directed by Pagnol.

1937 Original novel of *Regain*, directed by Pagnol.

1938 Original story of *La Femme du boulanger*, directed by Pagnol.

1948 Original play of *Le Bout de la route*, directed by Emile Couzinet.

1958 Scenario and dialogues (with Alain Allioux) of *L'Eau vive*, directed by François Villiers.

Scenario for *Le Foulard de Smyrne*, directed by François Villiers.

1959 Scenario for *La Duchesse*, directed by François Villiers.

1960 Scenario, dialogues, and direction of *Crésus*, with technical assistance of Claude Pinoteau.

1961 Scenario and commentary of *L'Art de vivre* photography by Paul Soulignac, directed by Edouard Berne.

1962 Original novel of *Les Grands Chemins*, directed by Christian Marquand with supervision of Roger Vadim.

1963 Scenario and dialogues for *Un Roi sans divertissement*, directed by François Leterrier.

1965 Original novel of *Le Chant du monde*, directed by Marcel Camus.

1966 Scenario and dialogues of *La Chevelure d'Atalante*, (TV version) directed by Robert Mazoyer.

1967 Scenario for *04*, directed by M. Serrin, screened as part of *Le Rampart des Béguines* of Guy Casaril.

1969 *Scenario of L'Etoile du Sud* (of Jules Verne), directed by Sydney Hayers.

1973 Original novel of *Le Déserteur* (TV version), directed by Alain Boudet.

André Malraux: 1901-1976

1939 Scenario, dialogues, and direction of *Sierra de Teruel (Espoir)*, with Spanish adaptation by Max Aub, titles by Denis Marion.

Alain Robbe-Grillet: 1922-

1961 Scenario and dialogues for *L'Année dernière à Marienbad*, directed by Alain Resnais.

1963 Scenario, dialogues, and direction of *L'Immortelle*.

1966 Scenario, dialogues, and direction of *Trans-Europ-Express*.

1968 Scenario, dialogues, and direction of *L'Homme qui ment*.

1971 Scenario, dialogues, and direction of *L'Eden et après*.
Scenario, dialogues, and direction of *N a pris les dés* (TV version of *L'Eden et après*).

1974 Scenario, dialogues, and direction of *Les Glissements progressifs du plaisir*.
Scenario, dialogues, and direction of *Le Jeu avec le feu*.

Marguerite Duras: 1914-

1957 Original novel of *This Angry Age (Un Barrage contre le Pacifique)*, directed by René Clément.

1959 Scenario and dialogues for *Hiroshima, mon amour*, directed by Alain Resnais.

1960 Scenario and dialogues (with Gérard Jarlot) for *Moderato Cantabile* directed by Peter Brook.

1961 Scenario and dialogues (with Gérard Jarlot) for *Une aussi longue absence*, directed by Henri Colpi.

1964 Scenario for *Nuit noire, Calcutta*, directed by M. Karmitz.

1965 Scenario for *Les Rideaux blancs*, directed by Georges Franju.

1966 Scenario, dialogues, and direction of *La Musica*, with technical assistance of Paul Séban.
Scenario and dialogues for *La Voleuse*, directed by Jean Chapot.

1967 Original novel of *The Sailor from Gibraltar (Le Marin de Gibraltar)*, directed by Tony Richardson.
Original novel of *10:30 P.M. Summer, (10h30 du soir en été)*, directed by Jules Dassin.

1969 Scenario, dialogues, and direction of *Détruire, dit-elle.*

1971 Scenario, dialogues, and direction of *Jaune le soleil* from *Abahn Sabana David.*

1972 Scenario, dialogues, and direction of *Nathalie Granger.*

1973 Scenario, dialogues, and direction of *La Femme du Gange.*

1975 Scenario, dialogues, and direction of *India Song.*

1976 Scenario, dialogues, and direction of *Son nom de Venise dans Calcutta désert* (sound track of *India Song*).

1977 Scenario, dialogues, and direction of *Des Journées entières dans les arbres.*
Scenario, dialogues, and direction of *Baxter, Vera Baxter.*
Scenario, dialogues, and direction of *Le Camion.*

1979 Scenario, dialogues, and direction of *Le Navire 'Night.'*
Scenario, dialogues, and direction of short films: *Césarée, Les mains négatives,* and *Aurélia Steiner* (2).

BIBLIOGRAPHY

General:

Bazin, André, "Théâtre et cinéma." *Esprit*, June 1951, pp. 891-905.

Bertin, Célia. "Romanciers-cinéastes." *La Revue de Paris*, April 1967, pp. 146-49.

Bluestone, George. *Novels into Film*. Berkeley, Calif.: University of California Press, 1961.

Brochier, Jean-Jacques. "De Flaubert à Minelli: les adaptations au cinéma." *Magazine Littéraire*, June 1970, pp. 8-31.

Elsen, Claude. "Qui est l'auteur d'un film?" *Ecrits de Paris*, November 1967, pp. 116-20.

Fell, John. *Film and the Narrative Tradition*. Norman, Okla.: University of Oklahoma Press, 1974.

Fuzellier, Etienne. *Cinéma et littérature*. Coll. 7e Art. Paris: Ed. du Cerf, 1964.

Geduld, Harry, ed. *Authors on Film*. Bloomington, Ind.: University of Indiana Press, 1972.

Kast, Pierre. "Film et roman." *Cahiers du Cinéma*, January 1967, pp. 12-13.

Magny, Claude-Edmonde. *The Age of the American Novel*. Trans. by E. Hochman. New York: Frederick Ungar Press, 1972.

Marcus, Fred. *Film and Literature*. Scranton, Pa.: Chandler Press, 1971.

Moeller, Hans-Bernhard. "Literature in the vicinity of the film: On German and *nouveau roman* authors." *Symposium*, Winter 1974, pp. 315-35.

Ollier, Claude and Jean-André Fieschi, eds. "Film et roman: Problèmes du récit." *Cahiers du Cinéma*, December 1966, pp. 3-129.

Richardson, Robert. *Literature and Film*. Bloomington, Ind.: University of Indiana Press, 1969.

Sadoul, Georges. *French Film*. New York: Arno Press, 1972.

Ropars-Wuilleumier, Marie-Claire. *De la Littérature au cinéma: Genèse d'une écriture*. Paris: Armand Colin, 1970.

______. "Pour un cinéma littéraire: Réflexions sur les possibilités actuelles de l'expression cinématographique." *Cahiers de l'Association des Etudes Françaises*, May 1968, pp. 223-37.

"Théâtre et cinéma." *Etudes Cinématographiques*. 6-7 (1960).

Jean Cocteau:

Alyn, Marc. "De la création littéraire et picturale au cinéma: Le visage et les masques de Jean Cocteau." *Le Figaro*, 14 November 1972, p. 30.

Amberg, George. "The Testament of Jean Cocteau." *Film Comment*, Winter 1971/1972, pp. 23-27.

Armes, Roy. *French Cinema since 1946*. 2 vols. London: Zwemmer, 1966.

Baroncelli, Jean de. "Un franc-tireur du cinéma." *Le Monde*, 13-14 October 1963, p. 15.

Beylie, Claude. "Cocteau." *Anthologie du Cinéma*, 12 February 1966, pp. 59-112.

Blistène, Marcel. "L'univers cinématographique de Jean Cocteau." *Les Annales*, April 1969, pp. 39-51.

Bory, Jean-Louis. "C comme Cocteau, c comme cinéma." *Cahiers Jean Cocteau*, 3. Paris: Gallimard, 1972, pp. 17-22.

Chalais, François. "Jean Cocteau et le cinéma." *Paris-Théâtre*, February 1954, pp. 15-17.

Chanel, Pierre. *Album Cocteau*. Paris: Henri-Veyrier-Tchou, 1975.

Charensol, Georges. "Cocteau et le cinématographe: Une âme mise à nu." *Nouvelles Littéraires*, 8-14 October 1973, pp. 15-16.

Cluny, Claude-Michel. "Le film est un autre langage." *Magazine Littéraire*, March 1970, pp. 23-25.

Cocteau, Jean. *"La Belle et la bête." L'Avant-Scène du Cinéma,* July-September 1973.

______. *Du Cinématographe*. Paris: Belfond, 1973.

______. "*Les Dames du Bois de Boulogne* (dialogues)." *Cahiers du Cinéma*, October-December 1957.

______. *Entretiens sur le cinématographe*. Paris: Belfond, 1973.

______. *L'Eternel Retour*. Paris: Nouvelles Editions Françaises, 1948.

______. "Notes sur *Le Testament d'Orphée*." *Cahiers du Cinéma*, June 1960, pp. 2-6.

______. *Orphée*. Paris: Ed. André Bonne, 1951.

______. *"La Princesse de Clèves." L'Avant-Scène du Cinéma*, April 1961.

______. *Ruy Blas*. Paris: Morihien, 1947.

______. *Le Sang d'un poète*. Paris: Ed. du Rocher, 1948.

______. *Le Testament d'Orphée*. Paris: Ed. du Rocher, 1960.

Crosland, Margaret. *Jean Cocteau*. London/New York: Peter Nevill, 1955.

Domarchi, Jean, and Laugier, Jean-Louis. "Entretiens avec Jean Cocteau." *Cahiers du Cinéma*, July 1960, pp. 1-20.

Doniol-Valcroze, Jacques et al. "Le chiffre sept." *Cahiers du Cinéma*, February 1964, p. 4-19.

Fowlie, Wallace. *Jean Cocteau: The History of a Poet's Age*. Bloomington, Ind.: University of Indiana Press, 1966.

Fraigneau, André. *Jean Cocteau par lui-même*. Paris: Ed. du Seuil, 1957.

Gilson, René. *Jean Cocteau*. Coll. Cinéma d'aujourd'hui. Paris: Seghers, 1964.

Hope-Wallace, Philip. "Jean Cocteau: Poet of the cinema." *The Listener*, 1 May 1952, pp. 718-19.

Kihm, Jean-Jacques. *Cocteau.* Paris: Gallimard, 1960.

Lambert, Gavin. "Cocteau and Orpheus." *Sequence*, Autumn 1950, pp. 20-32.

Langlois, Henri. "Jean Cocteau et le cinéma." *Cahiers Jean Cocteau*, 3. Paris: Gallimard, 1972, pp. 25-34.

Nogueira, Rui. "*Les Enfants terribles.*" *Melville on Melville.* London: Secker and Warburg, 1971, pp. 38-47.

Oxenhandler, Neal. "On Cocteau." *Film Quarterly*, Fall 1964, pp. 12-14.

______. "Poetry in Three Films of Jean Cocteau." *Yale French Studies* 17 (1956): 14-20.

______. *Scandal and Parade: The Theatre of Jean Cocteau.* New Brunswick, N.J.: Rutgers University Press, 1957.

Pillaudin, Roger. "Journal du *Testament d'Orphée.*" *Cahiers du Cinéma,* July 1960, pp. 21-33.

Renaud, Tristan. "Jean Cocteau. Un cinéaste? Peut-être. Un auteur? Certainement." *Cinéma '73*, December 1973, pp. 24-26.

R[ochereau], J. "Cinéaste des 'mythes en images'?" *La Croix*, 13-14 October 1963, p. 7.

Steegmuller, Francis. *Cocteau: A Biography.* Boston: Little, Brown and Co., 1970.

Tomek, James Joseph. "Relationship of Literature and Film in Cocteau." *Dissertation Abstracts International*, November 1974, pp. 3014-15A.

Sacha Guitry:

Bontemps, Jacques. "Une gravité enjouée." *Cahiers du Cinéma*, December 1965, pp. 103-9.

Gauteur, Claude. "Sacha Guitry et le cinéma." *Image et Son*, March 1971, pp. 3-8.

Gir, François. "Guitry au travail, par ses collaborateurs." *Cahiers du Cinéma*, December 1965, pp. 96-101.

LeGris, François. "Le théâtre, les films et les mots de Sacha Guitry." *Ecrits de Paris*, October 1959, pp. 108-17.

Lorcey, Jacques. *Sacha Guitry: raconté par les témoins de sa vie.*" Paris: Ed. France-Empire, 1976.

Madis, Alexis. *Sacha.* Paris: Ed. de l'Elan, 1950.

Marcorelles, Louis. "Sacha Guitry." *Sight and Sound*, Autumn 1957, p. 101.

Mars, François. "Citizen Sacha." *Cahiers du Cinéma*, October 1958, pp. 21-27.

Siclier, Jacques. "Sacha Guitry." *Anthologie du Cinéma*, 13 March 1966, pp. 115-68.

"Vive le théâtre filmé: entretien avec Sacha Guitry.' *Cahiers du Cinéma*, December 1965, pp. 88-91.

"La voix du maître: entretien avec Stéphane Prince." *Cahiers du Cinéma*, December 1965, pp. 92-95.

Marcel Pagnol:

Baroncelli, Jean de. "Un conteur du cinéma." *Le Monde*, 19 April 1974, p. 16.

Boussinot, Roger. "Marcel Pagnol." *Encyclopédie du Cinéma*. Paris: Bordas, pp. 1173-74.

Gauteur, Claude. "Marcel Pagnol, aujourd'hui." *L'Avant-Scène du Cinéma*, July-September 1970, pp. 7-8.

Gévaudan, Frantz. "Marcel Pagnol, un cinéaste mineur?" *Cinéma '74*, June 1974, pp. 11-13.

Guégan, Gérard. "L'importun du Midi." *Cahiers du Cinéma*, December 1965, p. 64.

Labarthe, André S. "Pagnol entre centre et absence." *Cahiers du Cinéma*, December 1965, pp. 67-71.

Leprohon, Pierre. "Marcel Pagnol." *Présences contemporaines*. Paris: Debresse, 1957, pp. 210-23.

Marmin, Michel. "Le cinéma selon Marcel Pagnol." *Le Spectacle du Monde*, June 1974, pp. 84-89.

Pagnol, Marcel. "Cinématurgie de Paris" (excerpts). *Cahiers du Cinéma*, December 1965, pp. 39-54.

______. "La crise du film français selon Marcel Pagnol." *Esprit*, February 1941, pp. 268-69.

"Sacha Guitry et Marcel Pagnol cinéastes malgré eux." *Cahiers du Cinéma*, December 1965, p. 22-23.

Vial, Fernand. "Provence and Provençals in the works of Marcel Pagnol." *The American Society of the Legion of Honor Magazine* 1 (1964): 29-47.

Jean Giono:
(see Marcel Pagnol also)

Beylie, Claude. "Giono revisité." *Marcel Pagnol*, Coll. Cinéma d'aujourd'hui. Paris: Seghers, 1974, pp. 59-74.

Chapier, Henry. "Jean Giono ou le cinéma pour veillées des chaumières." *Combat*, 24 August 1965, p. 6.

Chonez, Claudine. *Giono par lui-même*, Coll. Ecrivains de toujours. Paris: Ed. du Seuil, 1956.

______. "Giono rend Fernandel riche comme Crésus." *Les Nouvelles Littéraires*, 21 April 1960, p. 1.

Collet, Jean. "Magie de Giono." *Signes du Temps*, October 1963, p. 39.

Gauteur, Claude. "Giono et le cinéma." *Magazine Littéraire*, April 1973, p. 21.

Giono, Jean. "*Le Bout de la route*." *Théâtre de Jean Giono*. Paris: Gallimard, 1943.

______. *Crésus: Livre de Conduite du Metteur en Scène*. Manosque: Ricco, 1961.

______. "Le Foulard de Smyrne." *Bulletin des Amis de Jean Giono*, Autumn/Winter 1975, pp. 7-10.

______. *Les Grands Chemins.* Paris: Gallimard, 1948.

______. *Oeuvres Romanesques.* Coll. de la Pléiade, 3 vols. Paris: Gallimard, 1971, 1972, 1974.

______. "Préface de *Regain.*" *Regain.* Coll. Films qu'on peut lire. Paris/Marseilles: Ed. Marcel Pagnol, 1937.

Giono, Jean, and Allioux, Alain. *Hortense ou L'Eau vive.* Paris: Ed. France-Empire, 1958.

Godard, Jean-Luc. "Une fille nommée Durance." *Cahiers du Cinéma.* July 1958, p. 48.

"Jean Giono commence sa carrière de scénariste par un éreintement du cinéma." *Combat*, 23 August 1965, p. 7.

Laforterie, Jacques Gambier. "Le Hussard dans le tiroir." *France Film, Cinéma Nouveau*, March-May 1962, p. 4.

Mauriac, Claude. "Le Cinéma: *L'Eau vive.*" *Le Figaro Littéraire*, 28 June 1958, p. 18.

Meny, Jacques. *Jean Giono et le cinéma.* Paris: Ed. J. C. Simoën, 1978.

Pomerai, Odile de. "A Novelist turns to Films: Jean Giono and the Cinema." *Twentieth Century Literature*, July 1966, pp. 59-65.

Redfern, W. D. *The Private World of Jean Giono.* Oxford: Basil Blackwell, 1967.

Villiers, François. "Hommage à Jean Giono." *Le Figaro Littéraire*, 19-25 October 1970, p. 19.

André Malraux:

Agee, James. "Films." *The Nation*, 1 February 1947, p. 134-36.

Albersmeier, Franz-Josef. *André Malraux und der Film: Zur Rezeption des Films in Frankreich.* Bern: Herbert Lang, 1973.

___ . "Malraux et le Cinéma: Essai de Bibliographie." *Mélanges Malraux Miscellany*, Autumn 1972, pp. 3-24; addenda, Spring 1976, pp. 22-24.

Aragon, Louis. "Reconnaissances à André Malraux." *Ce Soir*, 12 August 1939, p. 3.

Barbarow, George. "The Malraux Film." *Politics*, March-April 1947, pp. 62-63.

Benson, Frederick R. *Writers in Arms: The Literary Impact of the Spanish Civil War.* New York: New York University Press, 1967.

Boak, Denis. *André Malraux.* Oxford: Clarendon Press, 1968.

Boussinot, Roger. *"Espoir." Encyclopédie du cinéma.* Paris: Bordas, 1967, pp. 531-32.

Carduner, Jean. *La Création romanesque chez Malraux.* Paris: Librairie A. G. Nizet, 1968.

Chantal, Suzanne. *Le Coeur battant.* Paris: Grasset, 1976.

Chazal, Robert. "*Espoir.*" *France-Soir*, 4 March 1970, p. 5.

Cuenca, Carlos F. *La Guerra de España y el Ciné*, 2 vols. Madrid: Editoria Nationale, 1972.

"*Espoir* (Sierra de Teruel)." *L'Avant-Scène du Cinéma*, May 1971, pp. 51-58.

Frank, Nino. "Le Cinéma: *Espoir*." *Spectateur*, 27 June 1945, pp. 1, 5.

Frohock, W. M. *André Malraux and the Tragic Imagination*. Stanford, Cal.: Stanford University Press, 1952.

Galant, Pierre. *Malraux: quel roman que sa vie*. Paris: Plon, 1971.

Garosci, Aldo. *Gli intellettali e la guerra de Spagna*. Turin: Einaudi, 1959.

Gubern, Román. "Filmografia sobre la guerra civil española." *Historia y vida*, March 1971, p. 101.

Hanrez, Marc, ed. *Les Ecrivains de la guerre d'Espagne*. Les Dossiers H. Paris: Pantheon Press, 1975.

Horvath, Violet. *André Malraux: The Human Adventure*. New York: New York University Press, 1969.

Ivens, Joris. *The Camera and I*. New York: International Publications, 1969.

Klaue, Wolfgang et al. *Filme contra Faschismus*. Berlin: Staatliches Filmarchiv, 1965.

Lacouture, Jean. *André Malraux*. Paris: Ed. du Seuil, 1973.

Lang, Serge. "*L'Espoir*, document humain." *Cinéma d'aujourd'hui*. Geneva: Trois Collines, 1945.

Langlois, Walter. "*Sierra de Teruel:* A Forgotten Treasure of the Library of Congress Film Collection." *The Quarterly Journal of the Library of Congress*, January 1973, pp. 2-18.

Leenhardt, Roger. "André Malraux et le cinéma." *Fontaine*, June 1945, pp. 403-5.

Louis, Robert; Segnaire, Julien; and Marion, Denis. "André Malraux, l'art et la guerre." *Magazine Littéraire*, October 1967, pp. 12-18.

Malraux, André. *L'Espoir* in *Romans*. Coll. de la Pléiade. Paris: Gallimard, 1947.

______. *Esquisse d'une psychologie du cinéma*. Paris: Gallimard, 1946.

______. "The Fascist Threat to Culture." Harvard University Address, Trans. by Ethel Saniel, 8 March 1937.

______. "Forging Man's Fate in Spain." *The Nation*, 20 March 1937, pp. 315-16.

______. "Réponse à l'enquête sur *Le Cuirassé Potemkine.*" *Revue Européenne,* May 1927, pp. 452-53.

______. *Sierra de Teruel*. Trans. and preface by Max Aub. Mexico City: Ediciones Era, 1968.

"Malraux: Dossier." *Magazine Littéraire*, September 1973, pp. 8-35.

"Man's Hope." *Time*, February 1947, p. 93.

Marion, Denis. *André Malraux*. Coll. Cinéma d'aujourd'hui, 65. Paris: Seghers, 1970.

______. "*L'Espoir*: film d'André Malraux." *La Nef*, June 1945, pp. 15-17.

Matignon, Renaud. "A 2: *Espoir* au ciné-club: Au carrefour de l'histoire." *Le Figaro*, 26 November 1976, p. 31.

Mauriac, Claude. "*Espoir* d'André Malraux." *Le Figaro Littéraire*, 2-8 March 1970, pp. 36-37.

______. "Il y a dix ans Malraux achevait *L'Espoir.*" *Le Figaro Littéraire*, 4 December, 1948, p. 6.

Michalczyk, John J. *André Malraux's Film* Espoir*: The Propaganda/Art Film and the Spanish Civil War.* (University, Miss.: Romance Monographs Inc., 1977.

Oms, Marcel. "Dossier-Film: *Sierra de Teruel.*" *Cahiers de la Cinémathèque*, January 1977, pp. 57-66.

Payne, Robert. *A Portrait of André Malraux*. Englewood Cliffs, N.J.: Prentice Hall, 1970.

Queval, Jean. "*Espoir.*" *Clartés*, 29 June 1945, p. 11.

Rougeul, Jean. "*L'Espoir* de Malraux." *Le Monde Illustré*, 30 June 1945, p. 29.

Siclier, Jacques. "Le regard de Malraux sur la guerre d'Espagne." *Cinéma*, 22 March 1970, pp. 56-57.

Thornberry, Robert S. "Malraux and *L'Espoir*: Propaganda and Beyond." *Malraux Mélanges Miscellany*, Spring/Autumn 1975, pp. 3-17.

______. *André Malraux et l'Espagne*. Geneva: Droz, 1977.

Vandégans, André. *La Jeunesse littéraire d'André Malraux*. Paris: Pauvert, 1964.

Vilar, Jean. "Un entretien avec André Malraux." *Magazine Littéraire*. July-August 1971, pp. 10-24.

Alain Robbe-Grillet:

Alter, Jean V. "Alain Robbe-Grillet and the 'cinematographic style.' " *Modern Language Journal*, October 1964, pp. 363-66.

Anzieu, Didier. "*Trans-Europ-Express* ou les jeux de la création cinématographique selon Robbe-Grillet." *Les Temps Modernes,* March 1967, pp. 1713-22.

Ashmore, Jerome. "Symbolism in *Marienbad.*" *The University Review* (Kansas City), Spring 1964, pp. 225-33.

Baby, Yvonne. "*L'Homme qui ment.*" *Le Monde*, 29 March 1968, p. 12.

Baroncelli, Jean de. "*L'Eden et après* d'Alain Robbe-Grillet." *Le Monde*, 25 April 1970, p. 11.

______. "*Trans-Europ-Express.*" *Le Monde*, 31 January 1967, p. 12.

Besses, Ona D. "A bibliographic essay on Alain Robbe-Grillet: Part III." *Bulletin of Bibliography*, July-September 1969, pp. 87-88.

Billard, Pierre. "Drogue, humour et *TEE*" *L'Express*, 23-29 January 1967, pp. 28-30.

"Biofilmographie d'Alain Robbe-Grillet." *L'Avant-Scène du Cinéma*, June 1974, pp. 68, 71.

Boisdeffre, Pierre de. "Robbe-Grillet, le nouveau roman et le cinéma." *A la Page*, December 1968, pp. 1786-96.

Brion, Marcel. "Alain Robbe-Grillet, un romancier réalisateur de film." May 1963, pp. 904-11.

Brunius, Jacques. "Every year at Marienbad." *Sight and Sound*, Summer 1962, pp. 122-27, 153.

Capelle, Anne. "Robbe-Grillet: mon dernier film." *La Quinzaine Littéraire*, 1-15 April 1968, pp. 24-25.

Capdenac, Michel, "Alain Robbe-Grillet: Le jeu de l'aventure, du mythe et de l'amour." *Les Lettres Françaises*, 27 January 1967, p. 18.

______. "Paradis, parodie." *Les Lettres Françaises*, 29 April 1970, p. 16.

Chalon, Jean. "L'Eden selon Robbe-Grillet." *Le Figaro Littéraire*, 13-19 April 1970, pp. 8-9.

Collet, Jean. "*Trans-Europ-Express* d'Alain Robbe-Grillet: Les voies de garage de l'intelligence." *Signes du Temps*, March 1967, pp. 31-32.

Doniol-Valcroze, Jacques. "Istanbul nous appartient." *Cahiers du Cinéma*, May 1963, p. 55.

Gardies, André. *Alain Robbe-Grillet*. Coll. Cinéma d'aujourd'hui, 70. Paris: Seghers, 1972.

G[odard], C[olette]. "Robbe-Grillet et le mythe de la cover girl." *Le Monde*, 26 February 1975, p. 23.

Holland, Norman. "Film, metafilm, and un-film." *Hudson Review*, Autumn 1962, pp. 406-12.

Houston, Penelope. "Resnais/Antonioni: *L'Année dernière à Marienbad* and *La Notte*." *Sight and Sound*, Winter 1961/1962, pp. 26-28.

Labarthe, André, and Rivette, Jacques. "Entretien avec Resnais et Robbe-Grillet." *Cahiers du Cinéma*, September 1961, pp. 1 ff.

Mason, Anne, and Danois, Michel. "Rencontre avec Robbe-Grillet, un vrai compliqué." *L'Aurore*, 18-19 April 1970.

Mauriac, Claude. "*L'Immortelle* de Robbe-Grillet." *Le Figaro Littéraire*, 30 March 1963, p. 20.

Montaigne, Pierre. "Robbe-Grillet entre la foudre et l'encens." *Le Figaro*, 18 February 1975, p. 24.

Morrissette, Bruce. "Problèmes du roman cinématographique." *Cahiers de l'Association Internationale des Etudes Françaises*, May 1968, pp. 275-89.

______. "Le roman et le cinéma: le cas de Robbe-Grillet." *Symposium*, Summer 1961, pp. 85-103.

______. *Les Romans de Robbe-Grillet*. Paris: Ed. de Minuit, 1963.

Oxenhandler, Neal. "*Marienbad* revisited." *Film Quarterly*, Fall 1963, pp. 30-35.

Parnell, Martin, ed. *Alain Robbe-Grillet*. Nottingham: Tarasque Press, 1968.

Pingaud, Bernard. "Le cinéma: Dans le labyrinthe." *Preuves*, October 1961, pp. 65-69.

Pivot, Bernard. "Michel Fano, producteur de *L'Immortelle:* Robbe-Grillet m'a ruiné... mais je ne regrette rien." *Le Figaro Littéraire*, 25 June 1964, p. 27.

Robbe-Grillet, Alain. *L'Année dernière à Marienbad*. Paris: Ed. de Minuit, 1961.

______. "Après *L'Eden et après*." *Le Nouvel Observateur*, 29 June 1970, p. 34.

______. *Colloque de Cerisy* (29 June-8 July 1975). Coll. 10/18. Paris: Union Générale d'Editions, 1976.

______. *Glissements progressifs du plaisir*. Paris: Ed. de Minuit, 1974.

______. *L'Immortelle*. Paris: Ed. de Minuit, 1963.

______. "Livre-film: La cover-girl du diable." *Le Nouvel Observateur*, 18-24 February 1974, pp. 54-55.

______. "Mes romans et mes films." *Magazine Littéraire*. April 1967, pp. 10-20.

______. "Le mot du metteur en scène: Jeux de l'initiation." *Le Figaro*, 15 April 1970, p. 30.

______. "Le nouveau cinéma et le nouveau roman." *Les Lettres Françaises*, 18-24 August 1960, pp. 1, 8.

Siclier, Jacques. "Deux cinéastes et l'érotique: *Les Glissements progressifs* d'Alain Robbe-Grillet." *Le Monde*, 7 February 1974, p. 17.

Sollers, Philippe. "Le rêve en plein jour." *La Nouvelle Revue Française*, May 1963, pp. 904-11.

Tisserand, J.-P. "De *Marienbad* à *L'Immortelle*: Robbe-Grillet renouvelle son écriture cinématographique." *Le Figaro Littéraire*, 1 September 1962, p. 9.

Tygal, S. "Alain Robbe-Grillet: pour un cinéma d'essai." *Les Lettres Françaises*, 24 September 1969, p. 16.

Ward, John. "Alain Robbe-Grillet: The Novelist as Director." *Sight and Sound*, Spring 1968, pp. 86-90.

Marguerite Duras:

Baroncelli, Jean de. "*Détruire, dit-elle* de Marguerite Duras." *Le Monde*, 17 December 1969, p. 10.

______. "*Des Journées entières dans les arbres*, de Marguerite Duras, *Le Monde*, 15 February 1977, p. 23.

______. *"La Musica* de Marguerite Duras." *Le Monde*, 7 March 1967, p. 24.

Barrault, Jean-Louis. "Silence et solitude." *Cahiers Renaud/Barrault*, 89 (1975), pp. 4-5.

Bernheim, Nicole Lise. *Marguerite Duras tourne un film*... Coll. Ça Cinéma. Paris: Ed. Albatros, 1974.

Billard, Pierre. "Resnais: Non, tu n'as rien vu . . . " *Cinéma '59*, July 1959, pp. 1-3.

Bontemps, Jacques. "Présentation de *La Musica*." *Cahiers du Cinéma*, February 1967, p. 42.

Canby, Vincent. "Marguerite Duras' *India Song*, a Four-Hankie Story." *New York Times*, 8 October 1975, p. 24.

Chapier, Henry. *"Des Journées entières dans les arbres* de Marguerite Duras: Une musique venue d'ailleurs." *Le Quotidien de Paris*, 9 February 1977, p. 13.

Cournot, Michel. "Marguerite-sur-Seine: *Aurélia Steiner*." *Le Nouvel Observateur*, 26 November 1979, p. 93.

Decoin, Didier. "Amende honorable." *Les Nouvelles Littéraires*, 14-20 January 1974, p. 4.

Delahaye, Michel. "*Détruire, dit-elle*." *Cahiers du Cinéma*, April 1970, pp. 60-61.

Devarrieux, Claire. "Marguerite Duras à propos du *Camion*: La voie du gai désespoir." *Le Monde*, 16 June 1977, p. 21.

Domarchi, Jean; Doniol-Valcroze, Jacques; et al. "Hiroshima, notre amour." *Cahiers du Cinéma*, July 1959, pp. 1-18.

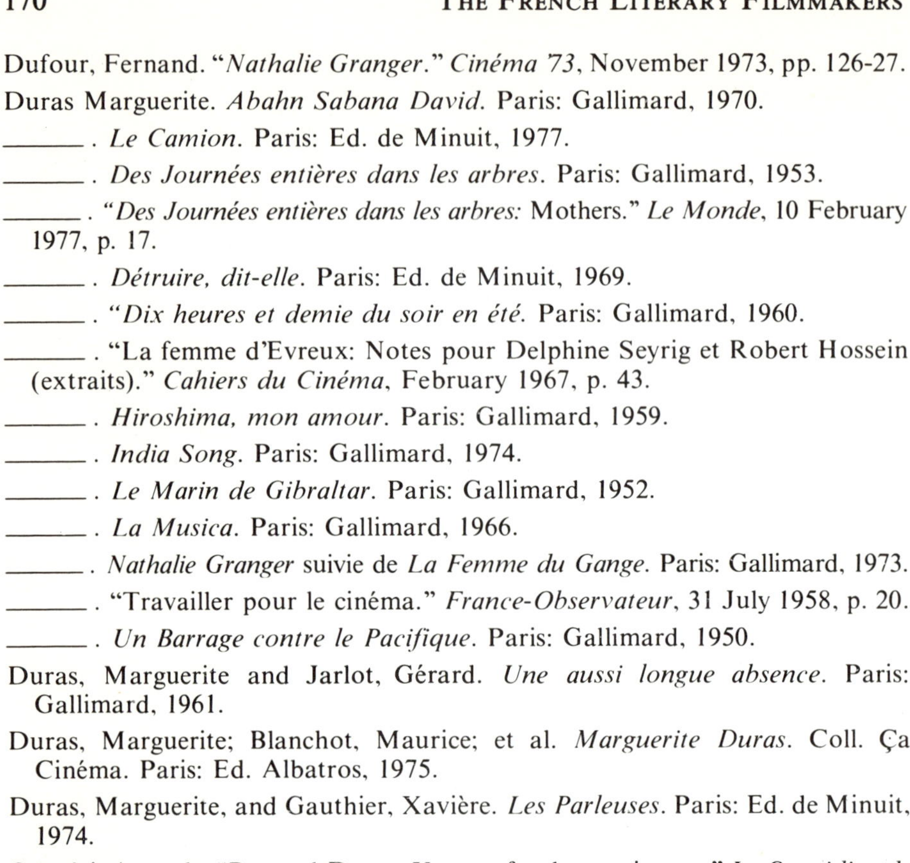

Dufour, Fernand. "*Nathalie Granger.*" *Cinéma 73*, November 1973, pp. 126-27.

Duras Marguerite. *Abahn Sabana David.* Paris: Gallimard, 1970.

______. *Le Camion.* Paris: Ed. de Minuit, 1977.

______. *Des Journées entières dans les arbres.* Paris: Gallimard, 1953.

______. "*Des Journées entières dans les arbres:* Mothers." *Le Monde*, 10 February 1977, p. 17.

______. *Détruire, dit-elle.* Paris: Ed. de Minuit, 1969.

______. "*Dix heures et demie du soir en été.* Paris: Gallimard, 1960.

______. "La femme d'Evreux: Notes pour Delphine Seyrig et Robert Hossein (extraits)." *Cahiers du Cinéma*, February 1967, p. 43.

______. *Hiroshima, mon amour.* Paris: Gallimard, 1959.

______. *India Song.* Paris: Gallimard, 1974.

______. *Le Marin de Gibraltar.* Paris: Gallimard, 1952.

______. *La Musica.* Paris: Gallimard, 1966.

______. *Nathalie Granger* suivie de *La Femme du Gange.* Paris: Gallimard, 1973.

______. "Travailler pour le cinéma." *France-Observateur*, 31 July 1958, p. 20.

______. *Un Barrage contre le Pacifique.* Paris: Gallimard, 1950.

Duras, Marguerite and Jarlot, Gérard. *Une aussi longue absence.* Paris: Gallimard, 1961.

Duras, Marguerite; Blanchot, Maurice; et al. *Marguerite Duras.* Coll. Ça Cinéma. Paris: Ed. Albatros, 1975.

Duras, Marguerite, and Gauthier, Xavière. *Les Parleuses.* Paris: Ed. de Minuit, 1974.

Gaspéri, Anne de. "Renaud-Duras: Une profonde connivence." *Le Quotidien de Paris*, 9 February 1977, p. 12.

Gousseland, Jack. "Le feu d'artifice de Marguerite Duras." *Le Point*, 14 February 1977, pp. 83-85.

Marcorelles, Louis. "Rebel with a camera." *Sight and Sound.* Winter 1959/1960, pp. 12-14.

Mauriac, Claude. "Le cinéma: Fluide amour, art volatil." *Le Figaro Littéraire*, 1-7 December 1969, pp. 37-38.

McWilliams, Dean. "The Novelist as Filmmaker: Marguerite Duras' *Destroy, She Said.*" *Literature/Film Quarterly*, Summer 1975, pp. 264-69.

"Mesdames les réalisatrices." *Cinéma Français*, June 1976, pp. 13-16.

Mohrt, Michel. "*Le Camion:* Haute voltige intellectuelle." *Le Figaro*, 18 May 1977, p. 24.

______. "*Des Journées entières dans les arbres*: Une admirable rigueur." *Le Figaro*, 12-13 February 1977, p. 19.

Montaigne, Pierre. "En direct de la Croisette: Le 'ras-le-bol' de Marguerite Duras." *Le Figaro*, 18 May 1977, p. 24.

"Portrait: Marguerite Duras." *Cinéma Français*, May 1970, pp. 47-51.

Rivette, Jacques; Duras, Marguerite; and Narboni, Jean. "Marguerite Duras: La destruction, la parole." *Cahiers du Cinéma*, November 1969, pp. 45-57.

Roud, Richard. "Conversation with Marguerite Duras." *Sight and Sound.* Winter 1959/1960, pp. 16-17.

Téchiné, André. "De trois films et d'une certaine parole." *Cahiers du Cinéma*, April 1967, pp. 48-51.

Vircondelet, Alain. *Marguerite Duras ou le temps de détruire*. Coll. Ecrivains d'hier et d'aujourd'hui. Paris: Seghers, 1972.

Wagner, Jean. *Le Navire 'Night'. Télérama*, 31 March 1979, p.91.

Zimmer, Christian. "Dans la nuit de M. Duras." *Les Temps Modernes.* February 1970, pp. 1304-13.

Index